D0565753

Praise for
I Don't Know What I Want, But I K

by Julie Jansen

"Is it possible to improve an already wonderful classic? Apparently it is, because that's exactly what Julie Jansen has done. This book could have saved me years of frustration at the start of my career!"
—Jon Acuff, *New York Times*–bestselling author of
Do Over: Rescue Monday, Reinvent Work & Never Get Stuck

"A superb guide for career changers that will definitely improve your life. Jansen provides the tools, insight, and support you need to evaluate yourself and to develop and implement an effective action plan to move on to a job you will love or at least like a lot."
—Robin Ryan, bestselling author of *60 Seconds & You're Hired*

"'Life-changing' is a bold claim. But with its inside-out approach to career creation, this book can be exactly that!"
—Bryan W. Mattimore, bestselling author of *21 Days to a Big Idea*

"A solid resource for people who know they don't like what they do; it might also be a wake-up call for others numbed into job complacency."
—*Publishers Weekly*

"A must-read for anyone who is working and feeling dissatisfied, unfulfilled, or unhappy with their current work situation."
—Paul Tieger, bestselling author of *Do What You Are*

"*I Don't Know What I Want, But I Know It's Not This* is the perfect guide if you want to find gratifying work but aren't sure how to get started. . . . Jansen includes lots of quizzes and questions to guide your look inward, but the best part of the book is the explanation of the answers, which helps translate your unique attitudes and values into a meaningful career. . . . Her handbook is a smart way to get going in a new direction."
—*BookPage*

PENGUIN BOOKS

I Don't Know What I Want, But I Know It's Not This

Julie Jansen has made five career changes within the broadcasting, contingency recruiting, outplacement, and training industries in order to find work that fulfills and satisfies her professional and personal needs. Since 1999, she has been coaching individuals to help them find jobs or change careers and consulting with companies to facilitate their employees' success at work. Jansen has been featured in publications such as the WSJ.com *Career Journal*, *Fortune*, FoxBusiness.com, *Psychology Today*, *New York Post*, and *U.S. News & World Report*, and she speaks, writes content, and gives career advice for *Cancer and Careers*. A frequent speaker for professional associations, nonprofit organizations, and corporations throughout the United States, she lives in Stamford, Connecticut.

For more information, visit the author's Web site at www.juliejansen.net.

I Don't Know What I Want, But I Know It's Not This

A Step-by-Step Guide
to Finding Gratifying Work

JULIE JANSEN

PENGUIN BOOKS

PENGUIN BOOKS

An imprint of Penguin Random House LLC
375 Hudson Street
New York, New York 10014
penguin.com

First published in Penguin Books 2003
First revised and updated edition published 2010
This second revised and updated edition published 2016

Copyright © 2003, 2010, 2016 by Julie Jansen
Penguin supports copyright. Copyright fuels creativity, encourages diverse voices, promotes free speech, and creates a vibrant culture. Thank you for buying an authorized edition of this book and for complying with copyright laws by not reproducing, scanning, or distributing any part of it in any form without permission. You are supporting writers and allowing Penguin to continue to publish books for every reader.

LIBRARY OF CONGRESS CATALOGING-IN-PUBLICATION DATA
Names: Jansen, Julie, author.
Title: I don't know what I want, but I know it's not this : a step-by-step
guide to finding gratifying work / Julie Jansen.
Description: Revised and updated edition. | New York, NY : Penguin Books,
2016. | Includes bibliographical references and index.
Identifiers: LCCN 2015032681 | ISBN 9780143128519
Subjects: LCSH: Career changes. | Job satisfaction. | Career development.
Classification: LCC HF5384 .J36 2016 | DDC 650.14—dc23 LC record available at
https://protect-us.mimecast.com/s/NV8GB7CMkE8Cx

Printed in the United States of America
3 5 7 9 10 8 6 4 2

Set in Adobe Garamond

While the author has made every effort to provide accurate telephone numbers, Internet addresses, and other contact information at the time of publication, neither the publisher nor the author assumes any responsibility for errors or for changes that occur after publication. Further, the publisher does not have any control over and does not assume any responsibility for author or third-party Web sites or their content.

This is dedicated to Zetta Bauer,
who died at ninety-six years old in 2014.
Momster, I miss your wisdom, unconditional love
and support, and humor every day.

Acknowledgments

For this third edition I am so grateful to:

Denise Marcil, who has always believed in the message of this book.

Meg Leder for your editorial talent and graciousness.

Shawn Belanger, Gail Harris, Shannon Kelly, and Anne Marie O'Farrell for your expertise.

My wonderful clients, who are generous in their appreciation and continual referrals of new clients.

Gary, my honey, for your amazing love and support.

All my readers—thank you, thank you, thank you!

Contents

Introduction

The first edition of *I Don't Know What I Want, But I Know It's Not This* was published in 2003. It is thirteen years later, and there are still so many people who aren't happy, fulfilled, or even moderately satisfied with their work.

According to the Economic Policy Institute, the Great Recession that lasted from December 2007 to June 2009 caused the US labor market to lose 8.4 million jobs, or 6.1 percent of all payroll employment, the most dramatic employment contraction of any recession since the Great Depression in 1929. Since 2009, the distribution of household income in the United States has become more disparate, with median household wealth falling by 35 percent. These events have created working environments filled with mistrust and uncertainty. For years after the Great Recession, people who were fortunate not to lose their jobs experienced increased workloads, zero or low salary increases, and even more limited opportunity for advancement.

While I was first writing this book and someone would ask me what it was about, I'd explain that it was about how to find satisfying work for the rest of your life. Without exception that person would say either "Wow, I sure could use your book right now!" or "My husband [friend/sister/son/cousin] desperately needs your book." Years later that refrain hasn't changed one bit, and the need for finding gratifying work is even greater. In fact, 52.3 percent of Americans were unhappy at work in 2014, according to the Conference Board, a New York–based nonprofit research group. What makes employees happiest at work? Being interested in their work, said 59 percent. What worries employees most: layoffs. While hiring has picked up considerably, only 46.6 percent of employees said they felt satisfied with their job security.

Some distinct changes have occurred in the workplace in the last decade, and among them is an even stronger need to define who you are (and aren't) and to find ways to brand yourself in your work. This means becoming well-known for something, whether it is a quality, a skill, or a specialty. Communicating what this is using social media has become both the norm and expected.

Another significant element of looking for a job, changing careers, and working in general is the necessity to be as resilient, nimble, and flexible as possible in order to meet the continuing extraordinary changes that are occurring in companies and in the workplace. Jason Alba, founder and CEO of JibberJobber, the leading online tool for organizing a job search, sums it up in this way: "In the near future we are all going to be contractors. Companies are treating employees like contractors, and this trend is strengthening. Like it or not, we will see our full-time job merely as one of many revenue streams."

Futurist Thomas Frey has predicted that more than two billion jobs will disappear by 2030, to be replaced by different jobs. For example, in the transportation industry, the world will begin to see driverless vehicles, which will eliminate bus, taxi, truck, and delivery drivers, while also creating a need for traffic designers, delivery dispatchers, architects, engineers, and managers of traffic-monitoring systems. According to a 2012 *New York Times* article called "Major Decisions," colleges and universities are preparing students for new careers by adding numerous new creative majors and encouraging students to graduate with double or triple majors, and with minors and concentrations, to become more specialized. This means that instead of simply majoring in business, students are taking on niche majors such as homeland security, culinary science/culinology, cyber forensics, casino management, and agro ecology. A World Future Society forecast that has become true in recent years is that professional knowledge becomes obsolete as quickly as it is acquired, at the fastest rate it ever has. This requires continuous instruction, education, and retraining for workers of all ages.

Finally, the development of a strong digital presence is a must as of the last decade. This means constantly updating your profiles on LinkedIn and other social media sites, writing blogs and commenting on blog posts, tweeting, and expanding and reaching out to your online connections regularly. However, it is also important to create the right impressions online, as it is nearly impossible to eliminate what has been coined "digital dirt."

I am in my fifth career, as a speaker, consultant, and career coach, which has made me even more intrigued by how and why people choose the work they do. I wrote this book to motivate others—to help them feel confident that being happy with work is a choice you *can* and *should* make. I empathize with those who are not happy or satisfied and have had difficult work experiences.

Why? I have had many myself. I have been fired, my job has been eliminated, I have had nasty bosses (two), and I have been caught in mergers and political battles. I have also worked for companies whose cultures were a bad fit for my needs, and I even had an ex-employer threaten to sue me because I had signed a noncompete clause preventing me from working in the same industry. I have been bored, disinterested, unchallenged, and miserable, as well as stimulated, engaged, and fulfilled. What did I learn from all these experiences? I learned that discovering the right work gives you motivation and confidence while you build a strong foundation. This enables you to bounce back and renew or even reinvent yourself when you need to do it. And you will need to do it!

This book will show you how to do all these things as you proceed on your journey to gratifying work.

PART I

Where Are You Now?

PART 1

Where Are You Now?

CHAPTER 1

Why Do You Want or Need to Change Your Work?

"I'm turning forty this year, and all of a sudden I'm questioning what I'm doing workwise. I've never had these feelings before. It's crazy!" says Kim, senior vice president of human resources at one of the largest banks in the United States.

Maybe you can identify with Kim's comment and her feelings of confusion about work. The workplace of today and what is predicted for the future certainly doesn't resemble the workplace that most people entered ten, fifteen, or thirty years ago. And it never will again. For a variety of reasons it has become increasingly difficult for most of us to feel satisfied with our work situation. Michael Leiter, a professor of occupational health at Acadia University in Nova Scotia, has studied burnout for many years. He believes that burnout is growing because of the push to work harder with fewer resources, less pay, and greater job insecurity. Additionally, technology allows the lines between work and home to blur, with no opportunity for respite.

The constant changes taking place in companies, including the temporary nature of jobs that were once relatively permanent, create a stressful work environment in which people find it difficult to feel satisfied, let alone happy. Endless communication (e-mail; instant messaging; texting; tweeting; voice mail; and phone, video conference, and in-person meetings), multiple projects with onerous deadlines, and extreme pressure to increase profits all contribute to an atmosphere in which many workers feel burned out.

In a study published in the online journal *PLOS ONE*, a nonprofit group that publishes medical and scientific research, three types of burnout were described: frenetic—feeling overloaded with work's demands or commitments; under-challenged—feeling a lack of development; and worn-out—wanting to neglect or give up one's tasks or responsibilities.

Debbie's situation fits the frenetic type of burnout. She sold nurse-call systems to hospitals for a giant health-care-solutions company. She felt so much stress from nonstop travel and unrealistic sales goals that she finally quit, taking a job that didn't have the same upside potential financially but also wouldn't be nearly as stressful. After giving notice at her former company, she spoke with ten or more individuals at various levels in the corporate hierarchy to say good-bye. She was shocked when every one of them told her that she was lucky to be able to quit, and if they felt they could leave their jobs, they would do so immediately. They made comments such as "It's not what it used to be" and "The company doesn't support us anymore; all they care about is profits."

"Burnout is not just about needing a vacation to recharge," explains Christina Maslach, professor emerita of psychology at the University of California, Berkeley. "It is when you feel overwhelming exhaustion, frustration, cynicism, and a sense of ineffectiveness or failure." Professor Maslach has researched burnout since the 1970s; in the early 1980s, she and her colleagues developed the Maslach Burnout Inventory (MBI), which has become a widely accepted method for assessing professional burnout. The inventory contains twenty-two elements in the areas of emotional exhaustion (chronic feelings of inability to face another day), cynicism or depersonalization (loss of idealism—having a negative, callous, or detached reaction), and reduced personal efficacy (a decline in feelings of competence and productivity at work).

Kim, the human resources executive mentioned earlier, works for a bank that recently acquired two large companies—the eighth acquisition in three years. The greatest problem posed by these acquisitions is the inability of the organization to successfully merge the disparate corporate cultures. This organizational stumbling block has resulted in higher employee turnover and confusion about shared values and goals. Not only has this affected Kim personally, but it has also required her, as a senior human resources executive, to deal with the serious repercussions that the mergers have on other employees.

Even though people know intellectually that hard work and loyalty aren't important to most employers the way they once were, it is difficult for many of us to accept it on an emotional level, especially by older generations. And the massive layoffs that occurred in the last recession have further diminished the loyalty employees of any age might once have had. Companies still aren't hesitant to lay off employees without warning.

Carol Sommerfield, PhD, is a career and organizational consultant who did her dissertation research on subjective underemployment, which is defined as "feelings that skills, talent, and education are not being fully utilized in one's job."[1] When she started her study in 2003, she had trouble finding any underemployed participants, as the economy was chugging along and people simply left jobs if they were unhappy. Now, almost all of her clients are subjectively underemployed, as salaries have dropped and benefits diminished, due in large part to the labor glut in the job market.

———

Many people are also feeling the stress brought on by multiple generations working together. In a 2013 survey by Lee Hecht Harrison,

———

1 Burris, 1983b; Jones-Johnson, 1990.

60 percent of employers reported experiencing intergenerational conflict of some kind. There are currently four generations working side by side in the workplace, each with conflicting values, attitudes, and expectations. Typically, traditionalists (those born in 1945 or earlier) see work as a necessity, baby boomers (those born between 1946 and 1964) believe in policies, procedures, and a chain of command as well as formal communication, Gen Xers (the generation born after the boomers, between 1965 and 1980) are independent and approach work with skepticism, pragmatism, and high expectations, and millennials (those born between 1981 and 1994, also known as Gen Yers) look at work as a place to find fulfillment and are constantly connecting, collaborating, and brainstorming digitally and socially. By 2020, these other generations will be joined by Generation Z (those born in 1995 and later, also known as the Net Generation or Digital Natives), who are also technologically savvy, fast-paced, creative, and collaborative.

Baby boomers, still a large generational employee group, have the highest level of disengagement in the US workforce, which poses a serious management problem for companies. The oldest baby boomers were approaching retirement age as the last economic crisis began, and many are delaying retirement to build up depleted savings, repay debt, or allow their portfolios to recover value. Other baby boomers simply prefer to keep working, either because they want to stay productive or because they are not sure how they would spend their time if they did stop working.

According to Gallup, traditionalists and millennials are the most engaged generations. While these two generations may share this characteristic, the difference between them is that millennials are also more prone to job-hopping if their needs aren't being met, which causes disruption in the workplace. Traditionalists, on the other hand, believe in staying put even if they are dissatisfied. Interestingly, this discord in attitudes and approaches to work between all four generations has become a major factor for workers to want to change careers. Unfortunately, companies don't tend to tailor goal-setting, incentives, and programs to improve communication or manage conflict between the generations.

Another factor that is causing stress in the workplace is intentional ageism by employers: Many people over the ages of forty or forty-five are feeling increasingly dissatisfied because they are experiencing either subtle or blatant discrimination from their employers. Joanie, at fifty-two, has sold advertising time in television for her entire career. When she was fifty years old, her boss stripped her of her national sales manager title and responsibilities, telling her, "You're fifty now and shouldn't be traveling as much." Many people in their forties and fifties believe that businesses are more interested in the young and technologically savvy worker. In particular, people who were laid off in their late forties and fifties are, in many instances, convinced that their age had a lot to do with the decision. People in this age range believe that companies, especially large corporations, perceive workers older than forty-five as less creative, less flexible, and more expensive than younger employees.

And, indeed, there is ample evidence that older employees are often replaced by young people who are willing to work like crazy. When these younger workers become managers, it can and often does lead to discomfort or outright conflict with older employees who once held these same jobs. The bottom line? Older employees often don't want to stay with companies where they are perceived in a negative light simply because of their age.

———

Yet another reason employees feel frustrated and dissatisfied is that many companies haven't yet embraced flexible work environments such as flextime, telecommuting, job-sharing, work-sharing, and compressed workweeks. People who've become frustrated with this lack of innovation are increasingly seeking out savvy companies that meet their employees' needs in this area. Ben, for example, designed audio equipment for a small company, commuting 112 miles every day for three years. Even though he could be very productive working in his home office, his employer didn't believe in telecommuting, thinking that if an employee wasn't in his company office, he wasn't working. Although Ben loved his job, his boss, and the company overall, at forty-seven he wanted to eliminate or at least reduce the stress of a long commute. He found a job with a larger audio company and now works from home. When he gave notice to his employers, in an attempt to keep him they grudgingly agreed to allow Ben to work at home once a week. While it was tempting to stay, Ben knew they never would fully support him, and he accepted the new job. As he anticipated, he feels healthier, and the stress created by driving a long distance to work every day is gone.

FlexJobs.com conducted a survey of fifteen hundred job seekers who were looking for flexible work arrangements. They found that 79 percent wanted to telecommute all the time, 47 percent wanted an alternative or flexible schedule, and 44 percent wanted to be able to telecommute part-time. Their reasons included work-life balance, family situations, health and exercise, time savings, reduced commute stress, and cost savings. They also believed that they could be more productive working from home, in large part because of reduced exposure to office politics and annoying colleagues.

In today's work climate, more and more individuals are questioning the grueling pace at which they lead their lives. The United States is the only developed country in the world that does not mandate vacation time. In 2013, Expedia surveyed more than eighty-five hundred people across five continents about their vacation practices. They found that Americans receive among the fewest vacation days (fourteen) in the world and also leave the most unused days (four) on the table. And according to a study conducted by the research company GfK for the US Travel Association in 2014, Americans exhibit a "work-martyr complex" by leaving vacation days on the table, citing the following reasons: they will return to a mountain of work, they feel that nobody else can do their work, or they are fearful that their employers will see them as replaceable. This work-martyr complex is often reinforced by company culture, as 67 percent of American employees say that their company says nothing about PTO (paid time off) or discourages them from using it.

Psychologically, the concept of introducing balance into one's life seems far-fetched and unrealistic for many workers. Why? The demands of today's workplace are excessive for most people. With technology allowing twenty-four-hour communication, employees feel obligated to work all the time, whether it be at night or on weekends or vacation. Even more important, many companies that have policies that support balance can give employees a mixed message about whether it is acceptable to leave the office at a reasonable hour or take all the vacation and personal time allotted in the company employee handbook. If senior management and the corporate culture demonstrate that succeeding means working around the clock, then the pressure of fitting in and "doing what it takes to get the job done" can override the desire to lead a balanced life.

Whitney is a classic example of someone who feels shackled by her employer's expectations about the amount of time employees need to work. She is employed by a large media company where the unspoken rule is that everyone must arrive at the office by 9:00 a.m. and cannot leave until 6:00 p.m., even if they are finished with their work for the day. Whitney and her husband want to start a family soon, and Whitney is concerned about having a newborn with a forty-five-minute commute and the pressure to adhere to the rigid hours.

In most cases, the challenge of creating a more balanced work life does not mean stopping work. Regardless of age, many of us feel that our sense of self is wrapped up in our work, and psychologically it would be difficult to stop working altogether, even if we could afford to do so financially.

The financial need to work is primary for most US workers. A 2014 paper by Accounting-Degree.org found that 35 percent of Americans over the age of sixty-five rely almost entirely on Social Security payments. According to the Congressional Budget Office, in 2010 the Social Security system began paying out more in benefits than it received. In 1950, sixteen US workers paid for each retiree's Social Security benefit; in 2010, 3.3 workers paid for each retiree's Social Security benefit; and by 2025, just two workers will fund each retiree. These statistics have a multitude of financial implications. People rely on Social Security, pensions, and personal savings to finance retirement. Accounting-Degree.org cites that six out of every ten working people in the United States are not confident that Social Security as we know it today will be able to pay benefits when they stop working. As for retirement plans, before the recession of 2008, 55 percent of Americans who were employed by companies were not covered by an employer-provided retirement plan. Projections show that corporations will be stopping 401(k) matches for those employees who are fortunate to have this benefit, and equity assets in retirement plans continue to drop dramatically.

In addition, baby boomers, who comprise the largest segment of the working population, are notorious for their poor saving habits, and a large percentage had their 401(k) plans decimated in the last major stock market decline. *USA Today* interviewed Jack VanDerhei, the coauthor of a 2014 Retirement Confidence Survey that found that 73 percent of those without a retirement plan such as an IRA, 401(k), or 403(b) have less than $1,000 in savings and investments. Retirement confidence exists mostly in people with higher incomes or those with retirement plans, VanDerhei explained. Because of this, many of us will find ourselves working longer and retiring later than previous generations.

People are also dissatisfied for reasons that don't necessarily have to do with the company they work for or the workplace overall. Instead, they have found themselves, either gradually or suddenly, feeling discontented or disenchanted with their work. Such feelings have more to do with the individuals themselves than with how they feel about their employer, and they may stem either from inner conflicts or from a longing for something different.

It is no longer true that the majority of people who question whether their values and goals are being met are middle-aged. Although many events that typically occur in midlife—such as the death of a parent, or a child leaving for college—may cause us to think more clearly about what is important to us, there is no age limit on searching for happiness and fulfillment in work and life. The overall uncertainty in the world along with perpetual change has caused many people in their twenties and thirties to examine what they need and want from work, especially if they saw their parents impacted by these things.

Although many employees are unhappy in their work, some of these people probably don't even know *why* they are unhappy, yet they acutely feel the symptoms of their discontent. These feelings can range from being depressed, bored, lethargic, and apathetic to being overwhelmed, stressed, or unchallenged. Those who do understand the reasons for their dissatisfaction are usually stuck; they find it easier to remain in an unhappy work situation than learn how to "unstick" themselves.

Work in the twenty-first century is dramatically different from the way it was in the 1960s, 1970s, 1980s, and 1990s. Engaging in a single career or lifelong trade is no longer the way we work or will work in the future. The US Department of Labor estimates that the average American will have three to five careers in his or her lifetime and ten to twelve jobs, and will hold each job an average of three and a half years. This means that changing careers is not only acceptable, it is also expected. Additionally, according to the Bureau of Labor Statistics, in 2014, 4.9 percent of Americans held more than one job, with half holding both a full-time and a part-time position. In an article in *Bloomberg News*, Bernard Baumohl, chief global economist at Economic Outlook Group, stated that the numbers are higher than government statistics reflect because of the fundamental changes in the labor market that have occurred since the recession and recovery of 2009. He explained that more people have entered and remained in the underground economy than ever before, meaning that workers are trying to raise their income by moonlighting and freelancing in response to real wages remaining stagnant years after the Great Recession.

The demands of the marketplace, as well as our personal lifestyle choices, dictate the kind of work we do and the way we structure it. Because of this, the capacity to shift gears more easily where work is concerned has become a critical skill for those intent on achieving a significant measure of life satisfaction. Learning to master this ability and make it your own will alleviate much of the discomfort and pain you may have experienced in the past or are feeling now.

Living is about making choices. Deciding what kind of work will make you happy is a choice—a big one. Today there are so many options that sometimes it may seem easier to sit still and not make any decisions at all. But it is clear: You can decide either to begin the process of change or continue doing something that isn't making you happy.

This book is about learning how to identify and create work that is right for you. The odds are that once you've read this book and have decided that you are ready and committed to change your work, you will look for a new job or career, and possibly leave the kind of work you've been doing for many years. Whatever you decide to do, there is one important point to bear in mind: Work is not "one size fits all." Your ability to make smart choices about the kind of work you do depends very much on who you are as an individual.

Every person I work with as a career coach feels unhappy or unfulfilled in his or her work or career. These people often tell me that many of their colleagues feel the same way, and while they believe that the job market is currently healthy, they know that looking for a job is much more complicated than it was the last time they conducted a job search. As a result, they are paralyzed or just not sure how to change or shift careers—so they don't. It is not abnormal or wrong to feel dissatisfied with work, but if you are feeling consistently negative about it, it is a mistake *not* to make changes.

Now it's time to move ahead and begin your journey toward a life of satisfying work!

CHAPTER 2

What Is Your Work Situation?

Six work situations represent a specific contemporary work-life challenge that you may be facing right now. Reading about these work situations will enable you to label and isolate the reasons for your desire to change your work and, in doing so, gain a clearer understanding of how to alleviate your dissatisfaction or discontent. While you probably will relate to one of the six work situations more than the others, it is highly likely that you will identify with two or three of them, or possibly even more. These situations are as follows:

1. *Where's the Meaning?* These individuals are looking for a new kind of reward and satisfaction. They may be seeking personal fulfillment or be driven by a strong desire to help others in need. Bill, for example, was an engineer for fifteen years but never really enjoyed his work. After being laid off by his company, a telephone equipment business, Bill took some time off and did volunteer work for five different organizations. He currently earns money by working several part-time jobs. His wife volunteers for many of the same organizations, and Bill tells me that they are both happier and having more fun than they ever had when they were earning substantially more money.

2. *Been There, Done That, but Still Need to Earn.* These people have been, and continue to be, successful in their work. They want and probably need to keep earning at the same level, yet they can't conceive of staying in the same job for another ten or twenty years. Many of these individuals won't be able to change careers immediately, but with planning they can do so eventually. A prime example is Melinda, who has worked in IT for most of her career. She stayed where she was for a while because she was making good money and because financial responsibilities precluded her from changing. When her children were older, she began to work as a personal fitness trainer at night and on weekends. Once Melinda's life situation changed (her children grew up, and she divorced her husband), she was able to launch full-time into her personal training business with established clients. Today she is making very close to the same amount of money doing something she enjoys.

3. *Bruised and Gun-shy.* These individuals are victims of the changing workplace. Having been laid off or discriminated against, they are hesitant to either join the corporate world again or take any kind of career risk, and yet they do need to continue working. Juan, after being laid off, had a quadruple bypass during the transition period and decided to become what he calls a "job stress coach." Ambivalent about reentering the corporate world, he now has his own practice helping others deal with the stress of working. In 2008 and 2009, enormous numbers of people were laid off from their jobs, and most of them remained unemployed months later. Fast-forward to 2016— many of these individuals were never able to find the level of jobs and incomes that matched what they had prior to being laid off.

4. *Bored and Plateaued.* Many people have worked hard for many years and are simply ready to make a change because they are bored and looking for new challenges. Deborah, at forty, had spent her entire career in consumer-products marketing. A vice president at an elite marketing firm, she admitted that she was "bored to tears." She remembered the early years of her career as being exciting and fun. For at least four years, however, she had felt stagnant, and finally she became so miserable that she decided to actively seek a new direction.

5. *Yearning to Be on Your Own.* These people dream of being on their own or starting a company. According to Helen Harkness, career author and futurist, in the early nineteenth century, 80 percent of Americans were self-employed. By 1970, this number had fallen to 9 percent. But in 2014, the Bureau of Labor Statistics (BLS) reported that 14.4 million Americans were self-employed. According to SBA.gov, privately held companies represented 99.7 percent of all employer firms. However, the BLS gets its data from the Current Population Survey, which excludes another type of self-employed group called "independent workers"—those who work temporarily on specific projects for many different companies. These comprised 17.7 million people in the United States in 2013. Independent workers don't have many of the responsibilities that a business owner has, yet they possess the flexibility that people experience in their own businesses. Some independent workers receive benefits, and some don't. With the increased stress of working for a company, more and more people are realizing that working on their own can satisfy their specific needs. After spending thirty successful years in teaching, sales, and human resources, Blanche started her own consulting firm several years ago. She says, "I always knew I wanted my own business and to have my stamp on something." She is having a lot of fun and has hit every goal she set for herself and her business.

6. *One Toe in the Retirement Pool.* These people are often baby boomers or traditionalists who want to semiretire or retire from their current work. What to do in the years ahead is a question that many of them are asking themselves: Do they change careers completely, volunteer, scale down the time they are working in their current job, or just retire completely? Di retired when she was fifty-eight from a long career in sales because her exhausting travel schedule was seriously affecting her health. During the first few years of her retirement she took yoga classes, read books, and learned how to paint in oils. Recently she has started doing some training seminars for a previous employer, and she is enjoying the combination of retirement and occasional part-time work.

Take a few moments and look at the descriptions of the six situations. The following list of questions and statements will help you identify your primary work situation, as well as the others that you fit within, and will provide you with additional clarity about why you associate with a specific circumstance. Taking this assessment may confirm what you already suspect about your reasons for being discontented with your work and allow you to gain further insights.

WHAT IS YOUR WORK SITUATION?

Read each statement carefully and answer yes or no as quickly and as easily as you can. The statements are grouped by work situation, and while you may think you fit into only one or two categories, you should answer all the statements to get a complete picture of your own circumstance.

WHERE'S THE MEANING?

1. In the last year or so, you have asked yourself, "Why am I doing the work I'm doing?" or "What is the point of the work I do?"

Yes   *No*

2. I'm not exactly sure what doing meaningful work means to me, but I'd be interested in finding out.

Yes   *No*

3. It is important that I directly touch or make a contribution to others as often as possible in my work.

Yes   *No*

4. I am feeling more and more that there is no reward or challenge for doing the work that I do.

Yes   *No*

5. I fantasize about "throwing in the towel" and going to work for a nonprofit organization or a specific cause.

Yes   *No*

6. There are several charities or special causes that I am very interested in learning more about and perhaps getting involved in, even simply as a volunteer.

Yes   *No*

7. My family and friends don't believe that I am making a difference in the world with my work.

Yes   *No*

8. I've experienced a traumatic or sad event in the recent past that has caused me to think about what is really important to me as a person in both my work and life.

Yes   *No*

9. I have an interest or hobby that I am passionate about and that I wish I could become more deeply involved with.

Yes   *No*

10. At one time it was important for me to meet my financial and achievement goals in my work, but this doesn't seem to matter to me anymore.

Yes   *No*

BEEN THERE, DONE THAT, BUT STILL NEED TO EARN

1. My work is no longer providing me with opportunities to do what matters to me, yet I'm used to my income.

Yes   *No*

2. I feel as if I have achieved a lot in my current career and would love to try a different kind of work but am afraid that then I wouldn't earn what I do now.

Yes   *No*

3. Earning the same amount of money or more is important to me so that I can take care of my family, but I am a little bored or dissatisfied in my job.

Yes   *No*

4. I really enjoy my work but feel as though I've had every possible experience in my career. Despite this, I honestly can't see changing careers because it would probably mean earning less money.

Yes   *No*

5. I have a lot of financial responsibilities that cause me to feel insecure about changing careers and earning less money.

Yes   *No*

6. While money is a big reason that I am afraid to change my work, if I think about it, I can find a realistic way to reduce or even eliminate my expenses in the next year or two.

Yes   *No*

7. I have grown used to my salary; however, if I sit down with a financial planner, I am sure I would learn that I can live on less money if this is what I need to do to change careers.

Yes   *No*

8. I must confess that the money that I earn is a huge part of my overall identity, and I am not sure I could see myself walking away from my paycheck for this reason.

Yes   *No*

BRUISED AND GUN-SHY

1. I had a tough job experience that caused me to lose my job and derail my career for a period of time, and I find it difficult to describe my experience or even think about it without feeling anger or other negative emotions.

Yes   *No*

2. I don't feel optimistic about the future of my career, in part because of my past negative work experiences.

Yes   *No*

3. I have been fired at least once. I still feel a little bitter about my experience, and although I'm not thrilled with my work situation, I don't think about making a change for fear it could happen again.

Yes   No

4. I am unemployed and can't seem to find the energy to focus on finding work that I enjoy, let alone a job of any kind.

Yes   No

5. I don't trust the corporate world anymore. When I started working, company loyalty was important. Joining a company meant you stayed there forever.

Yes   No

6. I've experienced some hard knocks in my career. I've been laid off, gotten caught in company politics, been discriminated against, and in one instance my company was sold. How much more do I have to take?

Yes   No

7. It seems that what companies want from their employees keeps changing. I just don't know if I can keep up the pace any longer, but I can't afford to stop working, either.

Yes   No

8. I've thought about becoming self-employed or changing careers, but I've been so burned that I'm afraid to make any changes.

Yes   No

BORED AND PLATEAUED

1. I've been working in the same job for more than two years without a change in responsibilities and can perform my tasks effortlessly without stretching myself.

Yes   No

2. I've invested a lot of time and energy in my work and am considered an expert in my field, yet I feel the need to change something about it, however minor that change may be.

Yes   *No*

3. I am so busy with tasks and projects that I don't have time to "smell the roses."

Yes   *No*

4. I have been having trouble getting out of bed in the morning, especially during the week, and feel unmotivated when I'm at work.

Yes   *No*

5. I daydream about quitting my job and doing something entirely different because I don't feel passionate about my work anymore.

Yes   *No*

6. At work I am experiencing feelings of burnout (anger, frustration, depression, and anxiety).

Yes   *No*

7. I guess after so many years in my field I should think about doing something different, but what would I do?

Yes   *No*

8. Although I know that my peers respect me, I'm starting to wonder if people think I still have passion for my job. In fact, I have been wondering that myself.

Yes   *No*

9. I moved from another company in my industry a few years ago in hopes that I would feel reinvigorated. I am starting to feel the way I did before I changed jobs—stale and unstimulated.

Yes   *No*

10. I've just begun to notice that I am not being included in important meetings regarding policy or strategy as often as I used to be. I feel as though I'm not contributing anything new, either.

Yes   No

11. Meetings, employees, and clients are all starting to look the same. This feeling scares me, but I'm not sure what to do about it.

Yes   No

YEARNING TO BE ON YOUR OWN

1. I no longer feel fulfilled working for someone else and don't think another job will give me what I'm missing now.

Yes   No

2. I am increasingly dissatisfied with the way the company I work for is run, and I'm convinced that I can do things differently and better.

Yes   No

3. I grew up in an entrepreneurial family or am close to someone who is an entrepreneur. I appreciate the advantages of having my own business more than I fear the disadvantages.

Yes   No

4. I'm so envious of people in their own businesses. I know it's not easy, but the thought of being my own boss is so appealing.

Yes   No

5. I've always dreamed of being in my own little business. I know there are plenty of resources out there for entrepreneurs, but I am not sure where or how to begin.

Yes   No

6. I know that being on my own doesn't have to mean starting a company. I would like to learn more about my options for self-employment because it is very attractive to me.

Yes   No

7. I know I want to go into business for myself someday but have never been a good salesperson. I'm afraid that not being comfortable with selling will cause me to fail.

Yes   No

8. I have thought a lot about the kind of work I'd like to do next, and I'm convinced that being an entrepreneur is my next move.

Yes   No

9. The idea of being a freelancer is incredibly appealing.

Yes   No

10. I'm very independent and have always had trouble with politics and working on teams. I am beginning to think that some form of being on my own makes sense for me.

Yes   No

ONE TOE IN THE RETIREMENT POOL

1. The truth is that I really would like to stop working right now. It just seems unrealistic to do so financially.

Yes   No

2. I never want to stop working completely, but I would like to slow my pace down a bit and do something different and less demanding.

Yes   No

3. I've been obsessing more and more about not working and spending more time with my family and with my hobbies and interests.

Yes   No

4. I'm stressed out from the demands of working and my health isn't what it should be. I'm seriously thinking about retirement.

Yes   No

5. I'm worn out from working. I've thought about my alternatives, and slowing down seems like the best one for me as long as I can work part-time.

Yes   *No*

6. I've worked for a long time and would welcome ideas about structuring the next phase of my life.

Yes   *No*

SCORE KEY

Place a check next to the categories in which you answered yes to four or more of the statements. Those are the work situations that describe how you feel about work right now.

☐ Where's the Meaning?
☐ Been There, Done That, but Still Need to Earn
☐ Bruised and Gun-shy
☐ Bored and Plateaued
☐ Yearning to Be on Your Own
☐ One Toe in the Retirement Pool

Now it's time to move forward and learn more about yourself and your preferences, needs, and desires—for your work and for your life. Once you have completed the self-assessments in chapters 3 and 4, you may choose to move through this book either sequentially or in a zigzag fashion. Each work situation is discussed in its own chapter with case studies of people who fall into the particular situation.

You will learn a three-step process for leaving your current work situation behind and moving toward something new or different, or merely changing aspects of your work to create what is missing.

Step 1: Complete the Self-Assessments
Specific to Your Work Situation

The first logical step to putting a plan together for your career is to learn and understand what your unique values, interests, personality preferences, attitudes, and favorite skills are. By using this information about yourself as a foundation, you'll be better able to focus your job search or career direction. Each of the six work situations requires additional assessments specific to your circumstance and the direction you'd like your career to take.

Step 2: Explore Roadblocks and Opportunities

Many obstacles and barriers may be preventing you from pursuing a different kind of occupation or changing the way you work—for example, age, money, time, education, and a lack of experience. On the positive side, the opportunities are limitless. In this step you will learn how to get around roadblocks and exploit your opportunities.

Step 3: Create an Action Plan

An action plan requires quite a bit of thought and preparation. While creating your plan requires a lot of time and energy, the action plan is an extremely valuable tool to use for mapping out a new career or revamping your career goals.

Although the journey that this book will take you on is not easy, it should be fascinating and eminently worthwhile. Ultimately, it will bring you to your desired destination: satisfying and fulfilling work for as long as you'd like to do it.

PART II

Where Do You Want to Be?

———

CHAPTER 3

Values, Attitudes, and Change Resilience

Whether you merely want to tweak your work situation or change it dramatically, it is essential that you get to know the one person who will be indispensable to your quest for work that fits: *you.* Understanding who you are—your values, attitudes, preferences, and personality traits—is the key to discovering the kind of work that will bring you personal fulfillment. Here is a simple analogy: If you invite friends over for a home-cooked dinner, you need to know exactly what ingredients to use in preparing the meal. When you throw in just any old ingredients, your guests will leave hungry and disappointed because the food you cooked tasted awful. Your values, personality traits, attitudes, and abilities are like the ingredients of a recipe. Without knowing what they are, you will find it difficult to help yourself create nourishing work.

A common mistake that many people make after deciding they are unhappy in their work is to jump immediately into updating their résumé and responding to postings on job boards, completely overlooking the first and very necessary step: self-assessment. According to psychologist Suzanne Roff-Wexler, director of Compass Point Consulting, LLC, a firm that specializes in career and organizational assessments, "With so many people dissatisfied with the work they do, it's more important than ever to think about job fit. Career assessments help begin an exploration process. There is no one direction for an individual, but some directions are just more viable than others. It often takes gathering more information and getting some help to make an advantageous change."

Bottom line? Don't skip this chapter or chapter 4! Read them, complete the assessments, and refer back to them as you read the rest of the book. In addition to helping you create your ideal work situation, the self-assessment process can help you uncover a whole new repertoire of words, phrases, and concepts that will add a rich new dimension to your résumé and job interviews. Not only will this make you feel more confident and prepared, but it will also have a positive effect on the people who meet you.

Assessment: What It Is and How It Is Used

"Assessment" is a generic term used to describe the various tests, questionnaires, quizzes, surveys, inventories, and checklists used by job search consultants, outplacement specialists, college counselors, career and executive coaches, and other career-management professionals to assist their clients. Using self-assessments will allow you to collect and evaluate your own preferences, experiences, values, needs, skills, and other personal traits. It is a foundation to help you identify or create the most suitable possible work opportunities for yourself. In other words, self-assessments help you find work that fits. Just imagine how productive the world would be if everyone who works found work that truly fit them.

The assessments in this chapter fall into three categories:

- Values
- Attitudes
- Change Resilience

Some people are fearful or intimidated by the assessment process because of what they may learn about themselves. Let's be perfectly clear: The assessments in this book are not psychological or clinical tests. In no way can a conclusion about your sanity or any personality dysfunction be ascertained from your answers. Self-assessments simply reaffirm what you already know about yourself—whether consciously or not—and provide you with a framework within which to pursue your quest for more satisfying work.

Joan has worked for several years in the search business for an agency recruiting and placing marketing professionals, and has been very happy in her work. Before this she worked as a senior administrative support professional. She truly believes that if she hadn't taken several self-assessment tests after being laid off from her last administrative position, she wouldn't be working in recruiting today. By completing the self-assessment process she was able to decide on a different direction for herself, one that she would never have considered otherwise. "Each person has a distinct personality and specific abilities that need to be guided toward possible career paths that are suitable for that person. When someone's decisions are based on these assessments, there will be a higher degree of success in a particular occupation; therefore, the result is greater fulfillment and happiness because the person is doing what he or she was meant to do in life. I'm living proof of this!" Joan says.

Let's begin your self-assessment process.

Values

A value is defined as a principle, standard, or quality considered inherently worthwhile or desirable. Individuals, groups, and whole societies hold values. Values are what motivate and fulfill you. They imbue your work and your life with meaning. Values can be either personal and non-work-related or completely work-related. In most cases, however, the values that are important to you will inform both your work life and your personal life. In essence, a value is what is important to you. While career psychologists have identified well over one hundred possible values, the list you are about to read contains forty-one values.

In this assessment you will first identify all the values that are important to you. You will then narrow down the list to your ten most important values. Last, you'll identify which of your top ten values are satisfied in your current work situation. This process will help you understand what is missing now so that you can be clear about what you're not willing to be without in the new work you choose.

Read the following list and place a check mark in the box to the left of each value that is important to you. Check as many as you like. Be careful not to check a value that you think "should" be of importance to you. Check only those you truly live by or are committed to living by in the future. For now, ignore the boxes on the right of each value.

LIST OF VALUES

☐ Achievement/accomplishment: producing results that are significant; completing tasks and projects successfully. ☐

☐ Advancement: consistently moving ahead to new and progressive opportunities. ☐

☐ Autonomy: ability to choose own projects, set own pace, prepare own schedule, and have own work habits with minimal supervision. ☐

☐ Balance: spending equivalent time and effort on tasks, work, and overall life. ☐

☐ Belonging to a group: having a sense of being a contributing member of a group. ☐

☐ Building something: creating or establishing a thing or idea. ☐

☐ Challenge: involvement with stimulating or demanding tasks or projects. ☐

☐ Competition: engaging in activities where results are measured frequently and compared with others'. ☐

☐ Creativity: making, inventing, or producing innovative, imaginative, or original things or ideas. ☐

☐ Doing good: contributing to the betterment of the world. ☐

☐ Entrepreneurship: organizing, managing, or starting a business or enterprise. ☐

☐ Equality: having the same capability, quantity, effect, value, or status as others. ☐

☐ Excitement: involvement with new and dynamic experiences with variety and change, and perhaps risk. ☐

☐ Fame: possessing extreme visibility or a great reputation; being recognized and renowned. ☐

☐ Family happiness: focusing on relationships, time spent with and attention given to children, spouse, parents, or relatives. ☐

☐ Financial security: pay and benefits that are satisfactory and predictable. ☐

☐ Friendship: frequent and caring relationships; camaraderie and interaction with others. ☐

☐ Fun: experiencing pleasure, amusement, and enjoyment. ☐

☐ Happiness: feeling or showing pleasure and satisfaction, contentment and well-being, joy and cheerfulness. ☐

☐ Harmony: feeling inner calm and tranquility; freedom from agitation, disturbance, or turmoil. ☐

☐ Health: optimal functioning of body, mind, and spirit. ☐

☐ Helping others: giving assistance, support, and aid to others. ☐

☐ Independence: self-reliance; freedom from the influence, guidance, or control of others. ☐

☐ Integrity: strict personal honesty; firm adherence to a moral code. ☐

☐ Leadership: guiding, motivating, developing, or directing others. ☐

☐ Learning: acquiring knowledge and satisfying curiosity. ☐

☐ Leisure: pursuing non-work-related activities. ☐

☐ Making a difference: causing a change in effect; changing the nature of something. ☐

☐ Personal development: challenging your capabilities; acquiring new skills and demonstrating abilities. ☐

☐ Physical activity: involvement in activities that rely on your body and physical exertion. ☐

☐ Recognition: being positively acknowledged by others; being given special notice or attention. ☐

☐ Respect: being treated with consideration and fairness. ☐

☐ Risk taking: facing unknown or dangerous challenges or demands. ☐

☐ Safety: freedom from danger, risk, or injury. ☐

☐ Security: protection from fear, anxiety, or danger; a guarantee of the fulfillment of an agreement; predictability. ☐

☐ Self-expression: ability to communicate or exhibit personal ideas, emotions, or feelings. ☐

☐ Spirituality: participating in a religious or ecclesiastical belief system; a sense of connection to something bigger than you. ☐

☐ Stability: maintaining an enduring, dependable, and predictable situation. ☐

☐ Status: possessing a prestigious or high-profile position or rank. ☐

☐ Teamwork: working closely with others toward common goals; having close working relationships. ☐

☐ Wealth: owning a significant quantity of money or possessions. ☐

If values that are important to you are not on the list of values, write them down on the blank lines here.

☐ _____ ☐

☐ _____ ☐

☐ _____ ☐

Now that you've selected all the values that are important to you, you'll narrow down the list to your top ten values. Read through your selections on the preceding list of values, and check the box to the right of any value that you absolutely cannot or will not live without. Ask yourself, "When I've been the happiest in my life, was this value fulfilled? Is this truly *my* value, or is it an unrealistic or unauthentic ideal that I really don't live by?" If you are unable to identify ten values, that's fine. However, do try to limit your number to a maximum of ten. In the spaces provided, write down your ten values in any order.

VALUE	YES	NO
1.	☐	☐
2.	☐	☐
3.	☐	☐
4.	☐	☐
5.	☐	☐
6.	☐	☐
7.	☐	☐
8.	☐	☐
9.	☐	☐
10.	☐	☐

Next, think about your current work situation. To the right of each value, check yes or no to indicate if this value is being expressed in any aspect of your work right now. Whether you are pursuing a different kind of work or simply trying to change the dynamics of your current career, it is very important to know which values are most significant to you.

Mary has a strong need for financial security and stability. These two values are fulfilled for her in her current job as an analyst for an investment bank. Two of her other values, however, are respect and balance, neither of which is being satisfied for her right now. Mary works with colleagues who are demanding and rude, and she consistently works sixty to seventy hours a week along with a three-hour daily commute. Mary really enjoys the kind of work she is doing and intends to look for a similar job in an industry other than investment banking. She plans on being very careful this time about assessing the culture of prospective employers to ascertain how employees work together and the ways that the company values its employees' time by supporting flextime, telecommuting, vacation, and reasonable deadlines.

By working for a company that does not support respect and balance, Mary learned the hard way about the values that are truly important to her. If Mary had known that respect and balance were so important to her, she would have asked probing questions during her interview in an attempt to understand the work environment.

You now have the benefit of learning what your primary values are so that as you move through the process of changing your work, you can keep your top ten list of values foremost in your mind. Continually refer to your list when you are analyzing and thinking about different work options.

Attitudes

Attitude is your state of mind or feelings with regard to a person, idea, or thing. Research has consistently shown that one's attitude directly motivates one's behavior. In a positive sense, those who possess an optimistic attitude about a goal or challenge are far better equipped to overcome any barriers to achieving that goal. On the other hand, an individual who has a negative attitude will find it much more difficult to achieve his or her goal. The process of assessing yourself and your work can be nerve-racking if you allow it to be. Self-assessment requires time, honesty, patience, and introspection. But even if you are willing to put in the time and effort, your overall attitude can "make or break" your ability to reach your goals.

This simple assessment focuses on your attitudes toward yourself and toward the external world as they pertain to work. For each statement, circle the word that most closely describes how you usually feel or act.

1. I have enough confidence in myself and my abilities that I am willing to take reasonable chances and do things I haven't done before in order to create satisfying work for myself.

Almost never   *Seldom*   *Sometimes*   *Frequently*   *Almost always*

2. I am uncomfortable promoting myself and think that if I'm doing a good job, the right people will notice.

Almost never   *Seldom*   *Sometimes*   *Frequently*   *Almost always*

3. I find that I really know the things I'm good at and not good at, and I think that self-evaluation is for people who are less experienced.

Not at all   *Seldom*   *Somewhat*   *Frequently*   *Almost always*

4. I feel that I put the maximum amount of time, energy, and enthusiasm into my work that I'm capable of doing.

Almost never   *Seldom*   *Sometimes*   *Frequently*   *Almost always*

5. I feel that relationships are very important to my career success and that I have developed and maintained strong relationships with people both within and outside my company and industry.

Almost never   *Seldom*   *Sometimes*   *Frequently*   *Almost always*

6. I initiate contact with my boss, my clients, and my subordinates consistently, offering support, feedback, and appreciation whenever possible.

Almost never   *Seldom*   *Sometimes*   *Frequently*   *Almost always*

7. Given the rapid pace of change and the excessive demands of employers and clients today, I don't believe that true job satisfaction is possible anymore.

Not at all   *Seldom*   *Somewhat*   *Frequently*   *Almost always*

8. When I have learned something new or make a meaningful contribution to my organization or industry, I document it immediately and then celebrate my success.

Almost never   *Seldom*   *Sometimes*   *Frequently*   *Almost always*

9. I set short-term goals for myself and include action items, which I take very seriously.

Almost never   *Seldom*   *Sometimes*   *Frequently*   *Almost always*

10. I am clear about my career goals and realize how important it is to have specific goals, monitor my own performance, and get myself back on track if I need to.

Almost never   *Seldom*   *Sometimes*   *Frequently*   *Almost always*

11. My job is so demanding that I am simply unable to get involved with professional development or keep up with reading the trade publications in my industry.

Almost never   *Seldom*   *Sometimes*   *Frequently*   *Almost always*

12. I work at keeping up-to-date on trends and other information about industries besides my own.

Almost never   *Seldom*   *Sometimes*   *Frequently*   *Almost always*

SCORE KEY

For each statement, match your answer with the numerical value listed. For example, if you answered Seldom for statement 1, your score is 2. Then add your scores as directed.

1. *Almost never*	*Seldom*	*Sometimes*	*Frequently*	*Almost always*
1	2	3	4	5

2. *Almost never*	*Seldom*	*Sometimes*	*Frequently*	*Almost always*
5	4	3	2	1

3. *Not at all*	*Seldom*	*Somewhat*	*Frequently*	*Almost always*
5	4	3	2	1

4. *Almost never*	*Seldom*	*Sometimes*	*Frequently*	*Almost always*
1	2	3	4	5

5. *Almost never*	*Seldom*	*Sometimes*	*Frequently*	*Almost always*
1	2	3	4	5

6. *Almost never*	*Seldom*	*Sometimes*	*Frequently*	*Almost always*
1	2	3	4	5

7. *Not at all*	*Seldom*	*Somewhat*	*Frequently*	*Almost always*
5	4	3	2	1

8. *Almost never*	*Seldom*	*Sometimes*	*Frequently*	*Almost always*
1	2	3	4	5

9. *Almost never*	*Seldom*	*Sometimes*	*Frequently*	*Almost always*
1	2	3	4	5

10. *Almost never*	*Seldom*	*Sometimes*	*Frequently*	*Almost always*
1	2	3	4	5

11. *Almost never*	*Seldom*	*Sometimes*	*Frequently*	*Almost always*
5	4	3	2	1

12. *Almost never*	*Seldom*	*Sometimes*	*Frequently*	*Almost always*
1	2	3	4	5

SCORE KEY

Add the total of scores for questions 1 and 2.

_____ This is your score for Self-confidence.

Add the total of scores for questions 3 and 4.

_____ This is your score for Self-knowledge.

Add the total of scores for questions 5 and 6.

_____ This is your score for Managing Relationships.

Add the total of scores for questions 7 and 8.

_____ This is your score for Maintaining Motivation.

Add the total of scores for questions 9 and 10.

_____ This is your score for Goal Orientation.

Add the total of scores for questions 11 and 12.

_____ This is your score for Professional Commitment.

WHAT DO YOUR SCORES MEAN?

Self-confidence

If your score for self-confidence is 6 or below, you may be feeling that your work has no value or that you are not appreciated by your employer. It may be that you are not taking any risks in your work or are not feeling optimistic and open. It is more difficult to make changes when your self-confidence is not healthy. Exploring and dealing with your reasons for lower self-confidence is important. Has something happened to you in the recent past that has caused your self-confidence to erode? Can you focus on achieving something that will improve your self-confidence?

Self-knowledge

If your score is 6 or below in this category, your assessment of yourself may not be as accurate as it could be. Honestly evaluating your strengths and the areas in which you may need more development as well as asking others for feedback may be useful exercises for you to undertake. If you are unrealistic about how well you really know yourself, then you will have difficulty identifying the best possible fit for yourself in relation to work.

Managing Relationships

A score of 6 or below in this category could indicate that you don't value relationships with others or that you have concerns about your effectiveness in dealing with other people. Networking is a crucial part of learning about the external world, and without strong relationships to help you, the process of exploration can be painful.

Maintaining Motivation

If you scored 6 or below in this category, it is possible that you have neglected your career. Staying focused and energized is up to you. If you aren't consistently thinking of ways to maintain your focus and energy where your career is concerned, you will have difficulty feeling motivated. This, in turn, will make it more difficult to achieve your goals.

Goal Orientation

If your score falls below 6 here, you probably don't have a focused plan of action for achieving specific outcomes. Setting reasonable yet challenging goals and really believing in them will help you keep motivated, especially when you want to do something different with your career.

Professional Commitment

It is likely that you are bored with your work or career if you scored below 6 in this category. Think about the reasons you entered your present line of work. What about it energizes you now or did so in the past? Your answer to this question may help you regain some of your sense of commitment to your profession. On the other hand, if you have difficulty coming up with a satisfactory answer, it may make sense for you to begin the process of changing the type of work you do.

If your work situation is less than desirable, your score may be low in one or several of these categories. Don't be overly concerned! Instead, think about why this is so and what you can do about it. Any of these areas can be developed with motivation, guidance, and the right tools.

Richard has been a photographer for twenty years and has grown increasingly unhappy with the way the photography business has changed. He isn't getting enough photo shoots to pay for his studio and support his family, and he realizes that he probably will have to close his business. Unfortunately, Richard's self-confidence has eroded so badly that he feels paralyzed about pursuing another career. In addition, he thinks that because he isn't good at networking or managing relationships, he won't be successful at uncovering new job opportunities. He isn't motivated to find a job and certainly doesn't have any kind of plan in place to move forward. Richard really needs to focus on each of these areas before he can move ahead in finding new work.

Your attitude as reflected by these six categories is something to be aware of as you think about changing your work. When you are happy and satisfied with your work, your score in each area will be very high.

Change Resilience

Most people don't like change. For many of us, change can be difficult or uncomfortable. This is true regardless of whether the change is forced upon us, planned, unexpected, or self-created. Why? Because we are giving up familiarity in exchange for the unfamiliar and unknown. When this occurs, we experience myriad emotions, including frustration, uncertainty, and fear. The classic book *Who Moved My Cheese?* by Spencer Johnson, MD, is a simple ninety-four-page parable offering a quick, easy, and fun way to understand change and deal with it quickly and effectively. Fear of change and what it represents is one of the reasons that people don't reevaluate their work. This assessment on change resilience is intended to help you increase your self-awareness about your comfort level with change. If you understand more clearly what your threshold of tolerance is for change, it will be easier for you to handle change and even make it happen. This is an important thing for you to know about yourself, because change is an unavoidable part of learning to find gratifying work.

When responding to the following statements, indicate how each one is true for you by placing the appropriate number in the blank to the left of the statement.

5 = *Definitely true*
4 = *Often true*
3 = *Somewhat true*
2 = *Scarcely true*
1 = *Almost never true*

____ 1. I can honestly describe myself as someone who seeks change regularly.

____ 2. I'm rarely surprised by changes at work because I usually see early warning signs and can prepare myself in advance.

____ 3. I am constantly trying to learn new skills even when there is no immediate need to do so in my job.

____ 4. When there is a change initiative going on within my company or with my clients, I am often asked by leadership to become involved in the process and implementation early on.

____ 5. I find it easy to look at a business problem from a different standpoint even if I haven't taken this approach in the past.

____ 6. When an employee or colleague suggests another way of handling something, I encourage him or her to try it even if someone else has already tried it this way in the past.

____ 7. I work very hard at staying current in my field by belonging to professional organizations, networking with people outside my company, and keeping up-to-date with industry blogs and trade publications.

____ 8. I look forward with great excitement to changing my work or career.

SCORE KEY

Add up the numbers that you entered for each question. Here is what these points indicate:

8 to 19 points	You have significant difficulty dealing with change. Change is simply not comfortable for you, and you tend to avoid it at almost all costs.
20 to 29 points	Although you are able to handle change under the right circumstances, you have to be highly motivated to instigate it.
30 to 40 points	Your ability to anticipate and handle change is admirable. You are usually adept at creating and responding to change.

Anyone can learn to deal more effectively with change if there are real reasons to do so and there is a reward for changing. If you are unhappy with your work situation, instigating and accepting change is very important in order to find satisfaction in your work. This is particularly true now that there is increasing pressure for many people to make significant changes. Whether you want to or not, this is a time when it is even more relevant for you to accept the need to change.

CHAPTER 4

Personality Preferences, Interests, and Favorite Skills

Now it's time to learn about who you are and what makes you unique, based on your individual characteristics and your personality, interests, and skills. The self-assessments in this chapter fall into three categories:

- Personality Preferences
- Interests
- Favorite Skills

Personality Preferences

Personality is the totality of an individual's distinctive traits. Although aspects of your personality can change slightly as a result of experience and self-awareness as you move through life, your inherent personality was developed by the time you were two years old. You cannot change the essence of who you are, but you *can* change your behavior. When you are looking for a good fit between who you are and the kind of work you do, it is important to know what your personality preferences are in order to ensure that they will mesh with your work.

Your personality encompasses many traits. The following statements assess some of the traits that have proved to be important when considering a career. There are no right or wrong answers when taking a personality preference test; however, it is important to respond quickly and intuitively. The statements may seem very black-and-white in nature, but this is intentional.

1. I like people for the most part; however, I prefer to work on my own.

Yes   *No*

2. When I enter a room filled with people I don't know, I feel shy and uncomfortable.

Yes   *No*

3. When I have to deal frequently with people on the phone or face-to-face, I feel drained by the end of the day.

Yes   *No*

4. I often think about what "could be" instead of what exists now.

Yes   *No*

5. New ideas, insights, and inferences really excite me.

Yes   *No*

6. I get bored very easily with projects that I'm working on.

Yes   *No*

7. I do not believe that it's very important to follow rules, regulations, and guidelines as closely as possible.

Yes   *No*

8. When involved in a business meeting or transaction, my first concern is how the other person feels.

Yes   *No*

9. I'm more likely to be described by others as "enthusiastic and warm" rather than "calm and cool."

Yes   *No*

10. When someone at work asks me to stop what I'm doing to help with a project, I feel disjointed.

Yes   *No*

11. I love schedules, definite deadlines, and planning.

Yes   *No*

12. I like having all the information before I begin a project and become uncomfortable when priorities change.

Yes   *No*

13. When I believe in something, I am not afraid to speak up even if everyone else disagrees with me.

Yes   *No*

14. I prefer to be the leader rather than have others lead.

Yes   *No*

15. I try very hard to get people to understand my way of thinking.

Yes   *No*

SCORE KEY

Write down the number of times you answered yes for the following sets of questions.

Questions 1 to 3
_____

Questions 4 to 6
_____

Questions 7 to 9
_____

Questions 10 to 12
_____

Questions 13 to 15
_____

WHAT DO YOUR SCORES MEAN?

Introverted or Outgoing

If you answered yes more often for questions 1 to 3, you tend to be more introverted. You enjoy your solitude, don't like being the center of attention, and typically work out problems and ideas by yourself.

If more of your answers are no, you are more outgoing and prefer to be with people more often than not. You probably have many social relationships and are expressive and easy to read.

Idealist or Realist

If you answered yes more often to questions 4 to 6, you prefer to imagine possibilities and are more of an idealist. This means that you love new ideas, insights, and inferences and tend to focus your energy on the future and what could be instead of what exists now.

If you answered no more often for questions 4 to 6, your focus tends to be more on reality and less on possibilities. You take things more literally, preferring the specific and realistic rather than what you can't see or have to imagine.

Emotional or Factual

Answering yes more often to questions 7 to 9 indicates that you are more emotional than factual. Being emotional means you tend to be more focused on feelings and your personal values.

If your answers are more often no, you prefer to be factual, veering toward analysis, laws, rules, and policies.

Structure or Spontaneity

If your answers are more often yes for questions 10 to 12, you like structure and prefer planning with fixed goals that have definite deadlines.

If your answers were mostly no for questions 10 to 12, you are spontaneous and prefer goals that are more open-ended. You tend to be flexible and adaptable to changing situations.

Assertive or Acquiescent

Answering yes more often to questions 13 to 15 means your personality preference is to be assertive. This means you tend to be more dominant and more of a go-getter.

If you answered no to two or more of questions 13 to 15, you are more acquiescent, tending to have a more passive nature and preferring to be behind the scenes rather than leading the pack.

How to Use This Information

Even when you are using skills in your work that you enjoy, and are interested in the work you are doing, if your personality doesn't match your work, you will not be satisfied. Kelly is an example. She is an introvert and a realist. She is emotional, acquiescent, and prefers structure. She works as a help desk professional, and while she enjoys information technology, Kelly goes home at night feeling exhausted by the constant barrage of phone calls and e-mails. She never seems to be able to accomplish what she sets out to do because she is constantly interrupted by requests for help from the employees of her company. Because she tends to acquiesce rather than lead, she isn't able to take control of her situation.

After you have taken the personality preference quiz, write down your preferences and compare them to your work environment to see if they fit. Let's see how Kelly's list looks.

PERSONALITY PREFERENCES	KELLY'S WORK ENVIRONMENT
Introverted	Deals with people constantly.
Realist	Kelly solves IT problems by collecting all the facts first even if it takes a long time.
Emotional	Kelly's boss and many of her colleagues focus on following rules and policies when making decisions.
Structure	There is a process that the employees of Kelly's company are supposed to follow when they need help, but this rarely happens.
Acquiescent	Kelly's passivity allows her colleagues to be demanding of her. She constantly feels pushed into a corner and often agrees to deadlines that are unrealistic because she feels uncomfortable setting limits.

Clearly, Kelly is working in a job that is not a fit for her personality preferences. Kelly would be much happier in an IT role in which she interacts with people in a more structured way and can stick to a schedule that is self-imposed rather than forced on her.

Now you try:

_____

_____

_____

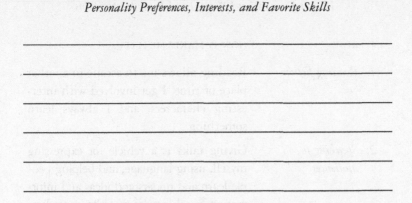

If you have completed your comparison of your personality preferences with your current work environment and have discovered, as Kelly has, that there isn't a strong match between the two, this could be a very good reason for your unhappiness in your work.

Interests

An interest is something that you are willing to give special attention to because you either feel strongly about the subject or you like the way it makes you feel when you are engaged with it. The degree to which you feel passionate about your interests can vary dramatically depending on your preferences with regard to the various topics or activities involved.

There are two steps to this first exercise. First, without thinking too intently, list ten activities or topics that interest you the most. They can be either work-related or non-work-related. Don't worry if you can't come up with ten.

Next, remembering your values and personality preferences, under the heading "How It Makes Me Feel" write down two or three words or phrases to the right of each interest that describe how that particular interest makes you feel or why it arouses a willingness on your part to involve yourself with it. Let me use myself as an example.

INTEREST	HOW IT MAKES ME FEEL
1. *Reading fiction*	Reading allows me to escape to another place or time. I get involved with interesting characters, and I always learn something.
2. *Speaking to audiences*	Giving talks is a vehicle for expressing myself, using language, and helping people learn and understand ideas and information. Speaking also provides immediate recognition.
3. *Watching movies*	The visual involvement with stories and characters makes me feel entertained and engaged.
4. *Organizing space or things*	Doing this appeals to my need for orderliness and makes me feel in control.
5. *Socializing one-on-one*	I get energy from people, and I'm very curious about others. It feels good to laugh, tell stories, and exchange information.
6. *Walking or sitting at the beach*	The beautiful environment and the sun relax me.
7. *Eating and drinking in restaurants*	I love the sensations involved with a social activity.
8. *Writing*	This is a meaningful venue for me to use language and help others.
9. *Giving advice and solving problems*	I like the intellectual challenge; I can make a difference.
10. *Riding on trains*	I like this speedy and efficient way to travel, and I find it relaxing.

Now you try:

INTEREST	HOW IT MAKES ME FEEL
1.	
2.	
3.	
4.	
5.	
6.	
7.	
8.	
9.	
10.	

Determining your primary interests is usually relatively easy, especially if you regularly spend time doing things such as playing golf or making stained-glass windows. What is difficult for most people is thinking about interests in relation to work. Many people tend to separate the two because they believe that they won't be able to fulfill their interests through work. Yet the people who are the most satisfied with their careers have found a way to tie their personal interests more closely to their work. This can mean creating more time outside of work to pursue their interests or working in a field or industry that involves their interests. Here are two examples: Barry works as a sales manager in the grass seed business. A major part of his job is playing golf—a sport that Barry is passionate about—with his clients, who are owners and managers of golf courses. Candace works in human resources, but her schedule is flexible enough that she can take two to three bike trips every year.

This assessment can help you think about how to relate your strongest interests to work. For example, I am a motivational speaker, an author, a résumé writer, and a coach. My work satisfies my interest in speaking to audiences, writing, giving advice and solving problems, and socializing one-on-one. I have often fantasized, however, about writing restaurant or movie reviews, which would combine my interests in writing, socializing one-on-one, watching movies, and eating and drinking in restaurants. Just because I love eating in restaurants does not mean that I want to own one or work in one. In fact, I did work in restaurants and disliked it.

Can you think of ways in which you can tie your interests into work based on the examples that have been provided? What are they?

_____

_____

_____

_____

_____

The next exercise is designed to help you understand your interest in specific types of work tasks and activities. Simply check the tasks and activities that appeal to you, regardless of the level of interest you have. You may or may not have tried these tasks before. For now, ignore the letter that follows each item.

___ Scheduling meetings	(D)
___ Counseling someone	(P)
___ Chopping wood	(O)
___ Participating on a sports team	(P)
___ Operating machinery	(O)
___ Planting flowers or a garden	(O)

___ Learning new software	(O)
___ Keeping records	(D)
___ Cooking food	(O)
___ Taking care of someone who is ill	(P)
___ Analyzing and managing investments	(D)
___ Negotiating a deal between two parties	(P)
___ Writing a business or sales proposal	(I)
___ Conducting research	(D)
___ Revamping a compensation plan	(D)
___ Handling customer complaints	(P)
___ Going on a sales call	(P)
___ Creating and editing a report	(D)
___ Organizing a desk	(I)
___ Teaching a class	(P)
___ Selling products in a store	(P)
___ Writing an article	(I)
___ Designing a Web site	(I)
___ Taking care of children	(P)
___ Farming organic vegetables	(O)
___ Preparing financial statements	(D)
___ Finding markets for new products	(I)
___ Interviewing a job applicant	(P)
___ Coordinating an event	(I)
___ Writing a press release	(I)
___ Repairing a watch	(O)
___ Planning a budget	(D)
___ Rewiring a house	(O)
___ Building a cabinet	(O)
___ Preparing accounting reports	(D)
___ Finding a new office space	(D)
___ Facilitating a meeting	(P)
___ Acting as a travel guide	(P)
___ Designing a costume	(I)
___ Opening new accounts for customers	(P)
___ Reviewing restaurants	(I)

___ Managing an employee team	(P)
___ Raising money for a cause	(P)
___ Creating Excel spreadsheets	(D)
___ Drawing maps	(O)
___ Fighting a fire	(O)
___ Analyzing census data	(D)
___ Writing a book	(I)
___ Reupholstering a couch	(O)
___ Decorating a house	(I)
___ Raising cattle	(O)
___ Designing a new business procedure	(D)
___ Conceptualizing a company vision	(I)
___ Creating a marketing campaign	(I)
___ Crowdfunding for a new product	(P)
___ Hosting a party to sell products	(P)
___ Maintaining golf course greens	(O)
___ Writing a blog	(I)
___ Analyzing insurance risk	(D)
___ Editing manuscripts	(I)
___ Reviewing legal contracts	(D)

Each of the tasks and activities listed falls into a specific type of interest category. The four categories are People, Ideas, Data, and Objects. Now look at the letter in parentheses next to each task or activity. Count the number of P's, I's, D's, and O's you have and write each number in the corresponding space below.

P ___

I ___

D ___

O ___

Read the definition of each interest category. The category with the highest number is your dominant interest.

People

You enjoy activities or tasks that involve a lot of interaction with people, whether individually or in groups. You may enjoy persuading, teaching, coaching, counseling, or directing people. Regardless, the key for you in your interests is to be involved with people the majority of your work time.

Ideas

This category involves theory, concepts, and the creation or expression of feelings, philosophy, or beliefs. You probably tend to lean toward the arts, music, drawing, painting, sewing, and writing.

Data

You are most interested in concrete and realistic tasks that involve schedules, numbers, financials, directions, procedures, and processes. You appreciate and are comfortable with the finite and practical nature of tasks or activities that fall into this category.

Objects

You like working with your hands, repairing things, and the precise and orderly use of machinery, tools, and inanimate objects. Working with plants and animals are part of this category.

Most people are primarily interested in one of these categories but enjoy and want to be involved with tasks in another category as well. Bernie, for example, loves his work in technical sales, yet has a degree in engineering and really gets involved in the design and installation of the equipment he sells. He's fortunate enough to be able to satisfy his interests in two distinctly different areas.

Favorite Skills

A skill is an ability or expertise. A favorite skill is a skill that you not only possess but are also *interested in* and *willing to use*. This is the difference between a skill and a favorite skill.

Although a skill can be defined as a broad category, like verbal reasoning or spatial relations, this assessment is focused on helping you understand how to identify specific skills that you can and want to use in your work, such as writing or scheduling, for example. We all have skills that we are good at but that we are not necessarily interested in using frequently or at all. While it is unrealistic to expect that you can avoid using certain skills without exception, it is not unreasonable to expect to spend the majority of your time at work using the abilities that you enjoy and are eager to use—your favorite skills.

For each skill or competency on the following list, you will assess two things:

1. What you believe is your degree of proficiency.
2. Whether you enjoy using it.

For degree of proficiency, use the scale provided and write the number that applies in the space to the right of the skill. For enjoyment, check those skills or competencies you enjoy using most in the space at the left. If you come across a particular skill that you haven't used in the past but think you'd enjoy using in the future, put an asterisk in the space at the left.

DEGREE OF PROFICIENCY

0—*Untested/never tried*
1—*Very limited*
2—*Below average*
3—*Average*
4—*Above average*
5—*Outstanding/mastery*

ENJOY MOST	DEGREE OF EXPERTISE
___ Writing business documents	____
___ Editing materials	____
___ Interviewing/hiring people	____
___ Mediating differences between people	____

___ Mentoring others
___ Negotiating deals
___ Public speaking
___ Facilitating a meeting
___ Presenting ideas
___ Coaching someone
___ Counseling someone
___ Teaching a class
___ Motivating people
___ Hiring someone
___ Leading a team
___ Training people
___ Helping others
___ Cataloging items
___ Handling scheduling
___ Keeping records
___ Conducting research
___ Evaluating ideas
___ Taking inventory
___ Setting standards
___ Assessing quality
___ Gathering data
___ Giving advice
___ Approving decisions
___ Delegating tasks/responsibility
___ Developing procedures
___ Managing people
___ Solving problems
___ Managing projects
___ Instigating change
___ Interpreting policy
___ Managing tasks
___ Analyzing budgets
___ Overseeing a profit-and-loss statement
___ Planning a budget

___ Doing cost accounting
___ Analyzing quantitative data
___ Creating a financial plan
___ Auditing
___ Developing policies
___ Conceptualizing new ideas
___ Developing strategy
___ Selling a product or service
___ Telemarketing
___ Creating a marketing plan
___ Writing proposals
___ Setting fee schedules
___ Creating an advertising campaign
___ Promoting a product or service
___ Coordinating events
___ Analyzing markets
___ Managing sales
___ Fund-raising
___ Serving customers
___ Handling customer complaints
___ Working with computers
___ Managing a large project
___ Designing technical products
___ Building something

Now, from your list, write down the ten favorite skills that you would most enjoy incorporating in your work (not necessarily in order of preference).

1.

2.

3.

4.

5.

6.

7.

8.

9.

10.

How many of your top ten favorite skills do you use in your current job? Which ones?

_____

_____

_____

How many of your strengths are above average or outstanding?

_____

_____

_____

Which ones could you develop more?

_____

_____

_____

Which ones haven't you tried before?

_____

_____

_____

_____

Getting to know yourself as well as you can is always an enlightening and useful process. In some instances your scores and results will merely confirm what you already know about yourself. In other cases you may be surprised by what you learn. Sometimes taking assessments will highlight ideas, assumptions, feelings, and strengths that you are aware of on some level but have not thought about in a long while or have kept submerged within your subconscious.

By going through the assessment process, you've taken an important and practical first step toward giving yourself insight into what kind of work will satisfy you. This, in turn, will help you devise an action plan and, ultimately, a solution for finding satisfying work. You will need to refer to your answers to all the self-assessments as you create action plans for your specific work situation.

Now you will move on to the chapters that describe the six categories you read about in chapter 2. Each chapter will provide you with a description of the specific situation, stories of people who fit into the category, and additional assessments that you can take to help you identify what to do next. Your challenge will be to discover what you can do to find, create, or change your current work to meet your needs. Once you have identified these things and are able to couple them with the confidence to make the adjustments that are needed, the process will be easier and more fun.

PART III

How Do You Get There?

CHAPTER 5

Where's the Meaning?

In a survey that I conducted of 110 people, more than 90 percent ranked "finding meaning" as the number one reason for why they recently had changed or would like to change their careers. The concept of "finding meaning" has so many interpretations that entire books have been written on the subject. The dictionary defines "meaning" as something that is signified or that has intent or purpose. To find meaning in work can denote being passionate about what you do and whom you do it for, or it can simply reflect your ability to set priorities in your work to satisfy your unique needs and desires. You may already know what meaning is for you, and you may realize that it doesn't exist in your work right now. Or you may not know exactly what meaning is for you, yet you know instinctively that it doesn't exist in your current work situation.

Despite being aware of the absence of meaning in their lives, some people never feel compelled to search for it. When it comes to work, it is much easier to focus on earning a paycheck to feed, clothe, and provide housing for yourself and your family than it is to examine your purpose and passion.

Every person is different; what is deeply meaningful to you may not matter in the least to someone else. The point is that to find meaning in your work you first must know what matters to you. And as you move through various phases in your life, the things that matter can often change.

Take the case of Chris. When the first edition of this book was published, Chris was a twenty-four-year-old administrative assistant at a television network, and meaning came from the knowledge that he was valued by his boss and coworkers for doing a good job. Even though the tasks he performed were essentially viewed as "grunt" work, he knew that he was needed. Chris was motivated by teamwork, recognition, respect, and learning. Chris knew that he wouldn't be doing entry-level administrative work forever, and his mature attitude enabled him to satisfy his need for meaning for the moment.

You may know what meaning is for you and realize that you don't have it, or you may not know exactly what it is but feel as if you don't have it. Nonetheless, one thing is certain: in order for you to find meaning, you need to be able to question the nature and purpose of the work you are doing now.

Step 1: Complete the "Where's the Meaning?" Self-Assessment

Before you learn how to incorporate meaning into your work, it is important to come up with your own personal definition of "meaning."

Your values are particularly important to understanding what meaning is to you. Remember that values are what fulfill you and motivate you. Go back to the list of values that you identified as most important to you on page 33 and review them.

Next, keeping your top ten values in mind, ask yourself the following questions and write down your answers.

1. When you think about the things you find meaningful, what comes to mind? Include things that are significant or important in your career as well as in your personal life. Your list of "things" should include ideals and feelings as well as activities.

_____

_____

_____

_____

2. Which of these things are you involved with now? Which
   have you done in the past? Which would you like to be
   involved with in the future? Be as specific as possible.

Past

_____

_____

Now

_____

_____

Future

_____

_____

_____

3. Take another look at your answers to questions 1 and 2 and narrow down your list. Be honest. Are there things on your list that you believe are meaningful but you know deep down that you'd never really pursue?

_____

_____

_____

_____

It is very important to find out what is actually meaningful for *you*. Understand that for one person meaning may be about spending more time with her children by shortening her commute and working from home one day a week, while for another it could mean reading to the visually impaired. Also be aware that the word "meaning" can be misconstrued to represent exalted ideals. In other words, meaning does not necessarily indicate that you are helping others or working for a charity.

Do not move on in this chapter if you are not clear about what meaning is for you. It is essential to know what you are working toward as you create a plan or learn how to overcome the obstacles to bringing meaning into your work.

One more point about knowing what is meaningful for you: Whatever you identify as having meaning for you today probably wasn't what was meaningful to you ten years ago and may not be so twenty years from now. What is relevant about the process of identifying and finding your meaning is that once you learn how to do it, the next time will be that much easier. Chris, the former administrative assistant we discussed on page 64, is now thirty-nine and works as an account director for a large technology company. When asked what is meaningful to him these days, his response is: "Helping others feel confident at work through teaching and coaching, camaraderie, a feeling of working together toward success, and working for a company that is doing good things in the world."

Now read the ten types of meaning and check the ones that are most important to you. You may feel that all ten types of meaning are important to you. If so, put an asterisk by the types that rank the highest in importance to you.

1. **Rewards and challenges:** something offered in exchange for service, to provide stimulation, renewal, or motivation (for example, money, awards, appreciation, applause, etc.). □

2. **Interesting field or industry:** work in an area of business that holds your attention or is somehow attractive, intriguing, or stimulating (for example, working in investment banking instead of commercial banking). □

3. **Expressing ideals and values:** live by or communicate standards, principles, or qualities (for example, working for a company that openly supports women and minorities). □

4. **Contributing/making a difference:** to give, share, or participate; to change or improve (for example, implementing a program that motivates and gives incentives to employees). □

5. **Solving problems:** answer questions or handle situations that present difficulty, uncertainty, or complexity (for example, working as a mediator). □

6. **Changing your lifestyle:** alter or modify your values, priorities, relationships, etc. (for example, work from your home office in order to spend more time with your children). □

7. **Feeling passionate:** experience powerful emotion or appetite (for example, work for a cause that you strongly believe in). □

8. **Supporting a cause:** contribute time, resources, or expertise; advocate for change on behalf of the cause; promote or advance the mission of a social or political movement or a needy or underserved population (for example, shift from a profit-making organization to a nonprofit). □

9. **Innovating/creating:** introduce, produce, or imagine something new or original that contributes in some way to the general good (for example, start a company that sells environmentally sound items for the home). □

10. **Learning:** to gain knowledge, understanding, or expertise through experience or study (for example, lead a new project in an area that you or your company hasn't been involved with previously). ☐

These ten categories will provide you with a broad foundation from which you can better identify and describe the types of meaning that are most important to you. Look back at your answers to the questions on pages 64–66. Which of these fit into the ten categories you just read? If, for example, one of your answers to question 1 on page 64 is "I started a new chapter of a professional association and increased the membership to 125 active members," a few of the categories of meaning that are important to you are contributing/making a difference, supporting a cause, and innovating/creating.

Analyze all your answers this way to see if the same types of meaning keep cropping up as the most significant to you. Did your answers to the questions on pages 64–66 align with the types of meaning you checked in the exercise on page 67 and this page as being important to you? As you move ahead in your quest for meaning in your work, refer back to the ten types of meaning and their descriptions, using them as a framework.

––––––––

Judi, who is in her early sixties, has had four careers. For twenty years she worked in sales. She has volunteered for various causes throughout her life and is often described by people who know her as a giving individual who cares about helping others. Judi loves sales, and she is very good at it. She has successfully sold telephones, real estate, marketing promotions, mortgages, and plush toys.

Despite her adjunct volunteer work and fondness for sales, Judi felt that she wanted to combine her avocation with her vocation and took a job selling assisted-living services. She believed that she finally had found her niche and was elated at being able to combine sales with something that held meaning for her. Then an opportunity to enter the field of fund-raising for a high-quality health system surfaced, and she decided to explore it. Judi said that fund-raising combined "my love of sales with a desire to touch people's hearts. It is an incredible feeling to be able to walk through a hospital, cancer center, rehab center, hospice residence, or nursing home and know that your efforts are supporting the services being provided to patients both in compensated and uncompensated care." When Judi and her husband, John, relocated to Kansas City from Connecticut because of the lower cost of living, after working in a few sales jobs, Judi went to work for the Kansas Department of Commerce, where she works with people whose jobs have been outsourced to a foreign nation. She assists them with finding training programs to retrain them as well as helping them to find employment. Not so coincidentally, many years ago as a volunteer, Judi cochaired a church-sponsored networking support group for the unemployed. She said she wished that she had realized earlier in her life that putting the meaning in her work was what she needed for professional fulfillment and that happiness in one's career is not derived from the money one earns or from successfully meeting targeted sales goals.

Step 2: Explore Roadblocks and Opportunities

Now you will identify any obstacles or barriers, either real or perceived, that could become actual roadblocks to finding your meaning. These are some examples: There isn't enough learning potential. I'm too old. I don't have a degree.

List them here:

_____

_____

_____

_____

Most of the barriers or obstacles you have written down may not actually be real but perceived. Here are some of the most common barriers that people believe would prevent them from changing their career to find more meaning.

"I'll have to take a decrease in pay."

This is the time to address the number one fear that people have about changing their career and/or industry: money! It is generally believed that if your brand of meaning involves working in the nonprofit world or if you switch to a new industry, you will have to take a significant decrease in pay. While it is common knowledge that the nonprofit world doesn't offer robust compensation packages, there is a valuable trade-off if making a difference or supporting a cause that is important to you.

Bruce is an excellent example. For twenty-five years he worked for a major New York City–based bank. He admits that of those twenty-five years he felt gratified for only eight—when he moved out of the audit and banking side of the business into an organizational development and training function. Yet even during those eight good years Bruce was never comfortable in banking but was constantly feeling that "I wasn't getting what I wanted—it wasn't ever right." When he was given the opportunity to take a separation package because the bank was merging with another bank, fearful as he was, he took it. He went through outplacement and during that time did, as he called it, "a lot of housecleaning." He took a hard look at his personal values and realized that a sense of mission and making a difference was something he craved—and that it had been missing for much of his career. One day Bruce attended a business luncheon meeting and listened to a panel of people who had successfully made the switch from the profit to the nonprofit world. Immediately, Bruce felt right at home. The proverbial "lightbulb" went on, and he knew that joining a nonprofit was clearly the path he needed to take.

After consulting for very little money or on a pro bono basis with various nonprofit organizations, Bruce was offered a job as chief financial officer of a New York City domestic violence agency. A victim of domestic violence himself while growing up, Bruce has never felt better or more fulfilled in his work. He is still number crunching but is also involved with strategy and wears innumerable other hats at the agency. He is earning less money than he did at the bank and admits that his ego was a little fragile about this at first. Nevertheless, he would never change his situation for a larger salary. If Bruce wants to, he can do consulting work on the side, write articles, and do many other things to generate extra income. Overall, his work life is less stressful, which gives him extra time and energy to pursue more of his outside interests.

As for the perception that you will have to accept less money if you switch careers, this really depends on how well you package yourself and your skills when you are "selling" yourself to potential employers or clients. Nici made a switch from being a marketing executive for an agency that worked with consumer products companies to a sales management position in the design field. Her current salary is comparable to her old one because she cleverly and effectively presented her management and marketing experience to her new employer. That and her obvious love of fashion and passionate interest in design easily convinced her new employer that Nici would be a great asset to the business.

"I'm too old."

While it is easy to look at certain fields or industries and fantasize about what it would be like to work in them—becoming a musician, an airline pilot, a sommelier, or an advertising executive—many of us stop ourselves from turning fantasy into reality by thinking of age as an obstacle. There are hundreds of stories about courageous individuals who dreamed of pursuing a career they had previously fantasized about and did it, despite being older. Even though the reality is that we live in a society that is biased against older people, the truth is that if you have the passion, drive, and courage to change your career at an advanced age, you can do it!

At the age of forty, with four children and limited previous work experience, Bernice went to law school. Her husband wasn't too thrilled about the idea at first, but Bernice was determined. While forty may not seem old to start a new career, most of Bernice's fellow law students were half her age. When she graduated from law school, Bernice worked for a law firm to gain experience and then started her own firm. Today she runs a successful law practice and has never been happier or more fulfilled. She gets deep satisfaction from making a difference in her clients' lives by fighting for their rights, whether in a real estate deal or a divorce. She thinks she is a better attorney now than she would have been had she gone to law school before or during the time she was raising a family simply because she's wiser and more mature now.

If you have written down "I'm too old" or "The corporate world discriminates against people my age," think again. These may be accurate statements if your dream is to become a pitcher for the New York Yankees or the hottest new model in Paris. There are always going to be companies and people in the world who favor youth in the workplace. But if you have the drive and have done your homework and learned about the industry you are passionate about, nothing should prevent you from becoming a part of it.

"I don't have specific industry experience."

You may believe that having little or no experience is something that can hold you back from going into a new industry. While you may not be familiar with the business you are interested in, you do have plenty of experience and skills from doing many other things. Business is business regardless of which industry you're in. There are always clients, customers, and stakeholders. Every business has sales, marketing, finance, human resources, product/service development, and operational needs. Goals and the need to achieve results are also standard issues in the business world.

Remember the ex-banker Bruce? While he was very interested in moving from profit to nonprofit, he didn't want to take the time to learn how to manage a nonprofit or become a fund-raiser because sales didn't interest him. Instead, he applied his accounting and finance skills to the nonprofit world. Yes, there was a slight learning curve for him, but it wasn't as dramatic as he had originally thought it would be. He was patient about finding the right nonprofit opportunity, first learning about the business while consulting and offering his services as a volunteer. When he stepped on board as CFO, he was ahead of the game from a knowledge standpoint. His employer appreciates the different perspective that Bruce brings to their operation and feels fortunate to have an ex-banker on his staff.

Learning about a new industry can be exciting and challenging, particularly if it is one that you've always thought about or leaned toward. Volunteering for a business, doing part-time consulting, interning, or sitting on a board or advisory council are wonderfully effective ways to get an education. There are companies that offer "returnships," a concept coined by Goldman Sachs to help ease the transition of high-potentials who have taken a hiatus or been out of work for a while back into the workplace. Every industry has trade publications and industry-specific associations that hold regular meetings and publish newsletters. The resources guide at the end of this book can help you identify some of them. Informational interviews are an excellent way to learn about a new industry. Networking with people to get the names of professionals who work in a specific industry, and compiling the same list of questions for each person, is a great information-gathering technique. Ask such questions as:

How did you get into this field?

What credentials, skills, and experience do you believe would be helpful for someone wishing to enter this field?

I've described my background and some of my major accomplishments to you. Which do you think are particularly transferable to your industry?

What are the most significant problems that you and people in your field are facing today?

When people see that you are passionate and have spent time trying to learn about their industry, they will be much more inclined to reveal opportunities and introduce you to decision makers.

"I don't know how to find a company that will allow me to express my ideals and values."

One of the obstacles you may face is your lack of knowledge about the type of industry, company, or environment that would support your values and ideals. Because you have taken the values self-assessment, you already know whether those values are being supported in your current work. If you hold tight to what is important to you, you will become more skilled at finding a work situation that will meet your needs in this area.

Ed is a perfect example. A human resource professional in his late forties, Ed had worked for a series of companies that failed to support diversity. As a gay man Ed constantly felt discomfort at having to work in an environment where he couldn't openly acknowledge his sexual preference. He also knew that his employer, a major investment house, was uncomfortable with the gay and lesbian communities. Ed's key value is to have the freedom to express his sexual preference openly. For the first time in his life he approached his job search with this important personal value uppermost in his mind.

Ed ended up at a smaller firm in the PR business that openly supports gay people in the workplace. How did he do it? He networked through a gay friend who is head of human resources at this firm. His friend persuaded the leadership to bring Ed on board in a higher-level human resources role than they originally thought they needed. By taking the time to find out what really matters to him and believing that it could happen, Ed landed a job that resonates with who he is as a person. Like Judi and Bruce and Bernice, he has never been happier or more fulfilled in his work.

When exploring companies or industries with an eye toward whether you'll be able to fulfill your values, you must ask tough questions and be prepared to accept the answers. In Ed's situation many firms professed to support diversity, but they really didn't—at least not to Ed's satisfaction. The better the job you do at investigating a company to find out whether its values and practices are really in sync with your own, the more likely it is that you will discover the truth. When trying to explore these types of concerns, ask questions such as:

How would you describe the corporate culture here?

Recognition is a value that is important to me. Can you give me examples of how the company recognizes its employees?

What are some reasons that employees succeed?

If a company resists having you talk to others besides their designated interviewing team, beware.

Sean worked for ten years as a very successful attorney with a large insurance conglomerate. While there, he was involved in a complex litigation matter, a massive refinancing, a sale of a significant business, and the purchase of an HMO. These projects sustained Sean well from the standpoint of professional challenge and the ability to contribute, solve problems, and creatively collaborate with colleagues and clients. Unfortunately, his employer's values began to change noticeably, and Sean felt as if the company he worked for was no longer in alignment with his own values and belief systems. His core belief in the importance of integrity, honesty, and family values had always motivated Sean to become involved in significant pro bono work, an activity that his company had always encouraged and even made possible for him to do, but now such opportunities were becoming scarcer. Although he was presented with many additional opportunities within the organization when he expressed his discontent to senior management, he chose to leave and became vice president of community relations for a real estate development company whose values supported his own.

"I can't make a difference."

Most human beings want to feel that they are either contributing to a greater cause or are having a positive impact on people or a process. One of the most common concerns people have is that although they would like to become involved in something where they will find this kind of meaning, they don't feel they can have a significant impact either financially or from an energy or time standpoint. Experiencing boredom in your job and feeling as if there is no meaning to your work are often connected.

If you are working in a job in which you don't feel as if you are really contributing or making a difference, take a look around you. What needs to be changed, improved, revitalized, or eliminated? Nothing is perfect, and there is always room for improvement or development. Make it your mission to undertake this kind of project. If the people you work with don't want this kind of help from you, then it may be time to look for a new work situation where you *can* make a difference. As Sean, the attorney who left the insurance industry, says of his new career in real estate, "I have the opportunity to combine and apply so many of my skills in the context of projects that make a real and substantial difference to communities."

You have special qualities, strengths, and skills that you enjoy using. Instead of thinking about what the world needs, reverse your thinking and identify the ways in which you can help a coworker, a group, a cause, or an organization by using your unique talents.

Janet is fifty-three and has had eight careers. She has been a teacher, an arbitrator, and a conservation technician in a museum, and she owned her own events company—to name a few. Currently, she works as the director of volunteers for a nonprofit agency for children. While doing volunteer work at the agency, she took a look around, thought about her skills and what she likes to do, and drew up a job description. She then approached the agency and convinced them that this role was needed and that she was the best candidate for it. Janet loves her job. "I work part-time," she explains. "I am continuing to build upon the experiences and skills that I brought to this position and am learning new skills at the same time. Perfect!"

"I'm not sure how I'll solve problems in an industry
I've never worked in before."

Sometimes you may not be sure that you are capable of solving a problem in an area in which you have no expertise or within an industry you don't know. The plus side of trying to solve problems in a field that is new to you is that you don't possess the habits and routine behavior patterns that often obscure the vision of someone who has worked closely in a particular industry. You can add a fresh perspective.

Gail had a long career in sales management for several large companies, and although she enjoyed it, she realized that she was tired of the day-to-day tedium of managing people. She decided to strike out on her own as a consultant working with privately held businesses. Gail always got excited about solving problems, and when she started helping small businesses solve their sales problems, she really felt as if she had found her niche.

"I don't know if I can change my lifestyle."

If you're like most people who work, you probably feel as if you don't have enough time in the day to get everything done either at work or in your personal life. You may even tend to push your family to the end of your to-do list in deference to your job and your boss. You may be exhausted, yet you just aren't sure how you can change the way you are living.

Howard was laid off from an executive job on Wall Street. After a month of not working, he commented to his outplacement counselor how impressed he was with his wife and children. He never knew who they were "as people" during his years of working on Wall Street and couldn't imagine ever letting his relationships with his family erode again. Although fearful that he wouldn't be able to earn the same amount of money, he researched franchises and bought one that sells juice to small companies. After a year and a half he was back to his old Wall Street salary. Sure, he had to work hard to build his business, but the flexibility he now has to spend time with his family has made a world of difference.

"I don't really feel passionate about anything."

If you have never truly felt passion for anything in your work, your greatest obstacle may well be finding out what it is that will give you this feeling. While it isn't necessary to be passionate, and most people aren't all the time, those who have taken the time to uncover their passion are truly happy, excited, and satisfied, and they view work in the same light as play. In *The Passion Plan*, Richard Chang outlines a seven-step model for bringing passion into your life. He describes passion as either content-based or context-based. Examples of content-based passion are activities such as golf, fishing, computers, and cooking, while context-based passions are centered on themes such as improvement, leadership, entrepreneurship, or competition. We can experience both types of passion in our work and in other areas.

While there may be something that you feel passionate about, if it is a hobby or an extracurricular activity, you probably think that it can't be woven into your work life. If you are a golfer, it is unrealistic to think that you can give up your day job and join the PGA TOUR! Yet you may be able to bring your passion for golf into your work. Frank, for example, works for a real estate management company. He manages buildings all over the United States and plays golf with half a dozen of the building managers. He has been able to combine earning a nice living with playing golf with his clients as often as he likes.

Think about what you feel passionate about. Is it something you are involved with outside of work? Is it something that you haven't been involved with in a long time? Is it something that you do at work but not enough to keep those passionate feelings ignited? Sit down with a piece of paper and write down all the ways that you can incorporate your passion into your work—forgetting for the moment any limitations that you may perceive. Or gather a small group of friends together and have a brainstorming session to generate ideas about how you can integrate passion into your work.

Not sure what your passion is? Start looking at the world through different eyes. What interests you that you've never done before? Is there an activity or hobby that you have always been drawn to but never tried? Why not find someone who does it and ask him or her to show you the ropes? Take a class or a workshop to see if it really turns you on. Whether you are interested in archery or running your own business, the only way to discover your passion is to try it!

Don waited until he retired to pursue his passion, which is teaching math to high school kids at a private school. He worked in corporate America for years and then sold insurance before "retiring" to teach math. "Yes! I am satisfied with my work," he says. "I wake up each morning looking forward to going to school. The students are challenging and fun to be with, and I love my subject."

"I don't have enough time."

While many of us fantasize about doing good and helping the less fortunate, we may also be thinking that there's not enough time to do so. In 2013, the US Bureau of Labor Statistics reported that 62.6 million people volunteered through or for an organization at least once in the previous year. If you increasingly feel the need to add meaning to your life by supporting a cause but also feel that you just don't have enough time to give, here are some suggestions.

To match your interests and skills with an organization in need of what you can offer, try looking at these Web sites: Volunteer Match.org and PointsOfLight.org. The resources guide at the back of this book also lists nonprofit and charity organizations that you can contact. If you are interested in supporting a cause and earning a living doing it, consider volunteer work first so that you can get a feeling for the way nonprofit organizations operate.

Of course, finding the time to volunteer is a real problem for people who work full-time. If you are someone who needs a more structured schedule, then commit to doing something at the same time every other week. If you prefer spontaneity, then volunteer for an organization that doesn't need you to be there consistently at the same place and the same time but is more interested in whatever effort or creative contribution you can provide. Start small, offering your time and talents in limited doses. If you work for an employer who supports programs in the community, get involved through this avenue first. Or approach your company and ask them to sponsor you in a volunteer effort by giving you flexible hours or time off.

Bill, who was introduced in chapter 2, was an engineer for fifteen years, and although he liked tinkering and was good at testing, he really didn't enjoy his work. He left engineering and moved into information services and general management in the telecommunications field. After five years he was laid off and took the summer to reflect on what he wanted to do. He and his wife, Merilee, had volunteered part-time for many years, and Merilee's career was already in the nonprofit sector. After a serious discussion with his wife, Bill decided to volunteer for a number of community organizations. Today he works as a volunteer ambulance attendant, a volunteer fireman, and a volunteer for a food-collection organization. He sits on the board of an agency that donates clothing and food to low-income families, works for a food bank, and is the chairperson of his church's Christmas tree sale. In addition, he loves to sing and is a member of a choral society and a male a cappella group. He generates income from three of these activities and says, "I'm fifty-six, and it seems that a lot of people I know are doing things that aren't making them happy. We, on the other hand, are having a lot of fun!"

"I'm not very creative."

As adults we can sometimes be apprehensive or feel insecure about our ability to be creative. We convince ourselves that creativity is only for children. But with technology taking over so many of our left-brain tasks, we have more of an opportunity to create and innovate. Unfortunately, we can get so mired in day-to-day tasks and deadlines that we don't make creativity a priority. We tell ourselves it's something that we will do when we "retire" or when we go on vacation.

Creativity takes so many forms—it's not just sculpting, painting, or writing. Julia Cameron's wonderful classic book *The Artist's Way* presents a step-by-step method for discovering and recovering your creative self. Cameron talks about taking your creative potential seriously by stopping negative talk such as "It's too late," "My friends and family will think I'm crazy," or "Creativity is a luxury, and I should be grateful for what I have." Although she wrote the book for aspiring and working artists, it is one that anyone can read to unleash the creative spirit lying dormant in all of us.

Creativity means being innovative, original, or imaginative. In the context of your current job, is there a way that you can focus more on these kinds of activities and less on the routine "business as usual" tasks? Do you have one idea that you've been thinking about for years but that you've never had the courage or taken the time to pursue?

Angie is a midlevel human resources professional at a nonprofit organization. While she fulfills her need for meaning, making a contribution, expressing her values, and supporting a cause very successfully in her job, she is constantly thinking of and inventing new products unrelated to her work. She has explored getting patents and manufacturing several of her innovations but always stops short of following through because of time, money, or family obligations. The next step for Angie should be to identify one invention and put a plan together to get a patent, find financing for manufacturing a demo of the product, and create a marketing plan. She can approach the Service Corps of Retired Executives, a nonprofit organization of retired executives who provide coaching to entrepreneurs. They can help her with the process so she doesn't have to pay someone for advice. Until Angie does these things, she will feel frustrated and unfulfilled despite the satisfaction she derives from her job.

Becoming the next Mozart, Rembrandt, or Shakespeare isn't what drives most people who seek to express themselves creatively, although feeling that you don't have the kind of talent those famous artists possessed may be impeding you. If you need to be more creative and innovative, the form or venue is irrelevant. What is relevant is the fact that you yearn to be more creative, and you should not wait until you have "the time or money" to do so.

"I'm not technologically savvy."

This is a statement that baby boomers in particular are guilty of repeating aloud over and over again. While it is true that Gen Xers and millennials were born in the Internet era and have used technology throughout their formative years, this doesn't mean that those of you who weren't can't embrace, accept, or simply learn how to use technology and the basics of social media. Employing various forms of digital communication simply means that you can reach more people and work more efficiently.

Instead of viewing technology as an overwhelming force you have to overcome, it is easier to look at it in small pieces. Do you want to use the computer for documents more often rather than handwriting them? Would it be easier to access and edit your calendar at the drop of a hat rather than writing it down in a book you carry? How about finding out what your doctor meant when he diagnosed your pesky health problem with a term you can't pronounce? Even if you can't spell it, just google it and hundreds of explanations will pop up.

An employer's expectation of employees' technological knowledge is that they possess a basic competence in a handful of software programs, such as Microsoft Excel, PowerPoint, or Outlook, all of which have been designed intuitively for the average user. While taking a class or reading a manual or one of the *For Dummies* books is helpful, every software program becomes easier to learn when you use it more frequently. Also, it is amazing how many hundreds of resources are available to ask questions and fix technology problems.

Technology doesn't have to be used only for work; it can be used for fun, too, and sometimes this is a simpler way to learn various types of technology. David, who worked in the insurance field, never used a computer until he retired at seventy. Now at age eighty-six, he Skypes with friends and family and plays poker on the Internet.

Step 3: Create an Action Plan

It's time to fill out a simple action plan to help you in your search for meaning in your work. Here is Angie's plan, to use as an example.

The kind of meaning I want to pursue is . . .
Innovating/creating: I'd like to sell my monogrammed selfie pole in catalogs and discount stores.

**The short-term action steps (tasks/activities)
I will take are . . .**

1. Contact the office of patents to learn about the process for securing a patent for my monogrammed selfie pole.

   When will I get this done? By April 15.

2. Contact the Service Corps of Retired Executives (SCORE) to find a counselor who can help me with my business plan for launching my monogrammed selfie pole.

   When will I get this done? By April 30.

3. Go through the steps of applying for a patent for my monogrammed selfie pole, filling out all the necessary paperwork and sending it in.

   When will I get this done? By June 30.

4. With the help of my SCORE adviser, write a business plan.

   When will I get this done? By July 31.

Now fill out your action plan. Although it may change based on the research you do or information you need, by putting your short-term goals on paper you will feel more committed to doing what you have to do in order to create the meaning you are yearning for in your work.

ACTION PLAN

The meaning I want to pursue is:

_____

_____

_____

_____

_____

The short-term action steps (tasks/activities) I will take are:

1. _____

   _____

   _____

   _____

   When will I get this done?_____

2. _____

   _____

   _____

   When will I get this done?_____

3. _____

   _____

   _____

   When will I get this done?_____

4. _____

   _____

_____

_____

When will I get this done?_____

Meaning is different for each of us. Without meaning in your work, whether it is one of the ten categories in this chapter or something that you've identified that isn't on the list, the only thing keeping you from finding it and making it happen is you. Whether it is a question of time, money, talent, attitude, drive, technical ability, knowledge, or interest—or your perception that any or all of these things can't or don't exist—there are plenty of resources to help you overcome your obstacles. Think about the kinds of meaning that are missing for you right now and start small by exploring how to add meaning to your work. Identify one thing that you can do, whether it's doing something creative, volunteering your time, researching an industry that you find interesting, or solving a problem that has been plaguing you at work. The joy and satisfaction awaiting you are indescribable.

CHAPTER 6

Been There, Done That, but Still Need to Earn

Tom is a vice president of human resources for a health-care contract research firm. At fifty-three he has made seven job changes since graduating from college, all within human resources. While he enjoys a large degree of independence, professional challenge, and satisfaction, he says, "I'd like the challenge of a new career. The reality is, however, that I am at a level both professionally and financially that is difficult to give up. That and the age of my children will likely keep me from pursuing an alternative career for another ten years."

If you are like Tom, this chapter is for you. You are enjoying a successful career but can't imagine continuing to do the kind of work that you've been doing for a long time. But—and there is a big "but" here—you really need to continue earning the same amount of money or more for a given period of time or even indefinitely.

Many people in the workforce feel the way Tom does. If you are one of them, take a leap of faith and buy into the philosophy that hope and possibilities exist *if* you uncover your true interests and are willing to begin to plan the next phase of your work. Yes, there is a next phase, but only if you believe there is and are willing to do whatever it takes to make it happen. If not, you will continue to sit in your job feeling stale and trapped.

Step 1: Complete the "Been There, Done That, but Still Need to Earn" Self-Assessment

First, create a new folder in your computer labeled "The Work I'm Going to Do Next" and keep it on your desktop, not hidden away in your archive folders! You'll need it to be easily accessible so that you can refer to it later.

Go back and look at the results of all the self-assessments you took in chapters 3 and 4. Begin by reviewing the values self-assessment on pages 30–33.

Now do the same with the attitudes self-assessment on pages 35–39. Are there one or two areas that you can work on within this self-assessment? Review the six categories within the attitude self-assessment. On the lines provided below, write down what you think you can do to improve your attitude in each category, keeping in mind the values that are important to you. I've made some suggestions to help you get started. Being proactive about shifting your attitude will help you jump-start the process of moving out of your Been There, Done That, but Still Need to Earn situation.

Self-confidence

In what ways can you improve your self-confidence?

Suggestion: Focus on one skill, such as networking, and practice it. Identify three new people you can meet. Call them and schedule a phone call or face-to-face meeting.

_____

_____

_____

_____

Self-knowledge

How can you improve your self-knowledge?

Suggestion: Ask three people who know you from different aspects of your life for feedback about something specific, such as the way you present yourself.

_____

_____

_____

_____

Managing Relationships

In what ways can you better manage your relationships?

Suggestion: Talk to a client, a friend, and your child or spouse about your relationships and what they'd like to get from them that they may not be getting now.

_____

_____

_____

_____

Maintaining Motivation

How can you better maintain your motivation?

Suggestion: Set a reasonable goal for yourself for something that you need to change or improve, such as time management or organization. Put a simple plan together with a time line for completing your plan. Document your progress.

_____

_____

Goal Orientation

How can you make yourself more goal-oriented?

Suggestion: Set one simple goal, such as finishing this book or writing a blog post once a week.

Professional Commitment

In what ways can you deepen your professional commitment?

Suggestion: Read two industry-related blogs in the next five days. Share one piece of information with someone else in your company or field.

Now review your results for the rest of the self-assessments you took, including your score on the change resilience quiz (page 41), your personality preferences (page 46), what your primary interests are (page 54), and your favorite skills (page 56).

Write down any and all titles, jobs, types of work, names of companies, and industries where you think you could possibly fulfill your values, top interests, personality preferences, and favorite skills. Use brainstorming techniques to do this: Write down as many ideas as come to your mind, whether they seem realistic or not. Try not to allow biases, prejudices, perceptions, or even concrete obstacles to negatively color your brainstorming process. Keep writing down words and phrases until you have run out of ideas. List them one by one on each line.

For example, Leslie, someone who is just beginning her self-assessment process, wrote, "Disney, MTV, Christie's (auction house), Amazon, museums, interior decorator, my own business, author, architect, nonprofit, teach kids art, botanical gardens, travel writer, chef."

_____

_____

_____

_____

_____

_____

_____

_____

_____

_____

Now you are going to prioritize your thoughts and ideas based on *your level of interest*.

1. Rank every single word or phrase that you've written by placing a large number next to it on the left side, starting with number 1. Once again, don't think about your prejudices, lack of knowledge, or

negative perceptions while you are prioritizing. Go with your gut. Don't spend too much time thinking about this exercise—just do it.

2. Do the same thing again, only this time write the number on the right side. Rank your words and phrases based on *how realistic it is that you can make this idea happen* (with the number 1 representing the most realistic).

In the second exercise, do not think about realism in the context of the present. Frame it in terms of "someday." By doing this you will avoid assessing the "realism" factor in terms of your ability to meet your current personal expenses. On the other hand, the amount of money you have to spend to make your goal happen *is* part of the realism factor. Let's say, for example, you wrote down "Buy a seat on the New York Stock Exchange." In 2006, the exchange entered into an agreement to merge with Archipelago and became a for-profit, publicly traded company, and "seats" were no longer available to buy. Now the NYSE sells one-year licenses to trade directly on the exchange for $40,000. Therefore, while your interest level may be high, your realism ranking may not be because of the high cost of entry and the limited availability of licenses.

When you finish these exercises, review your lists carefully and look for any surprises or common themes. What are they? Do the job titles, industries, and work you prioritized as your top five interests match any of the five that led the list when you prioritized them from a reality perspective?

Now look at your list of top values, interests, and motivated abilities from the assessment you took and compare it to your top five job, industry, or work interests. Based on the knowledge you have, will these things provide you with what you want and need? We'll come back to this later in the chapter.

Step 2: Explore Roadblocks and Opportunities

Having a career plan in place—with practical, achievable goals—significantly increases the probability of realizing those goals. Otherwise, you might sit and stagnate for another two or three years.

Let's explore the financial aspects of your situation. As Tony Robbins says in his book *Money Master the Game*, "What matters is that you master money and it doesn't master you. Then you are free to live life on your own terms." If you are dealing with exorbitant expenses, undoubtedly this is creating stress for you and your family. Revisiting your finances to learn where you can make sensible changes can only help to relieve this stress.

Start by making an appointment with a financial adviser. Be sure to find one through a referral from someone whose judgment you trust. Also be sure to choose someone who is truly skilled at putting a plan together for you and is not just interested in selling stocks or mutual funds. Be prepared to fill out a "net cash-flow form" that shows your monthly expenses and income. A good financial adviser will also help you understand your net worth and comprehend your tax situation more clearly. While you may have met with a financial adviser in the past, or have investments for which you receive advice, it is unlikely that you have ever *tied financial planning into your career* before. Most people tend to keep these two very important aspects of their lives separate until something happens, such as the sudden loss of a job. You need to know which of your assets and financial investments you will be able to use in order to finance a new venture, such as starting a business or changing careers.

If the top five jobs or industries you elicited from your brainstorming session are not at all related to your current job, then you probably aren't assured of being able to earn at your current level. In fact, most people automatically assume that if they switch industries or start a business, they will have to accept a drastic cut in pay. This doesn't always turn out to be true, however, but whether it's true or not, knowing you will disappoint yourself if you don't make a career change at some point, it's time for you to become familiar with your expenses, cash flow, and entire financial picture so that you can plan accordingly.

Some expenses, such as college tuition and alimony payments, are fixed for a definite period of time. Others, such as special education and treatment for a disability or an elderly parent in an assisted-living residence, are more difficult to plug into a time frame. Regardless of the categories that your expenses fall into, you should tell your financial adviser that you intend to change careers. He or she will help you set financial goals aligned with your needs so that you can make a financially sound change.

Remember Tom, the human resources executive who believed that being financially responsible for his children would prevent him from pursuing a new career for another ten years? In ten years Tom will be sixty-three, and while many people are still vibrant and interested in learning new things at that age, Tom's energy and his career interests will be dramatically different by then.

If you are like Tom, what should you do? In addition to completing the assessment at the opening of the chapter and consulting with a financial adviser, you should also examine the less tangible aspects of money. What are your attitudes toward it? How important is earning a good salary to you, beyond your financial responsibility to your family? In her many books, financial expert Suze Orman hones in on these "softer" aspects of dealing with money, helping readers become aware of how they were raised to think about dealing with money and what is at the root of their specific financial habits, such as spending and saving.

If you haven't already done so, review the options available to you for reconfiguring your present job. Go through the exercise of writing down every one of the jobs you have held since college and identify three things:

1. Your level of satisfaction in the role and the reasons for it (whether you were satisfied or not).
2. Your greatest one or two accomplishments while in each position.
3. The strengths and skills you learned and used to achieve these accomplishments.

Once you have identified these things, you will see some consistent themes for what makes you feel happy and satisfied in your work, and what does not. Write down these themes and then look at your current position and think about ways you can increase the factors that bring you job satisfaction or how to find them without changing jobs.

You should also do what many people do: look at ways to fulfill your interests outside your job. Eventually, an outside interest or activity can turn into a full-time job—with pay!

Sue is a good example of this. For seven years she has worked as a public relations coordinator for a nonprofit organization. When she had been in her full-time position for about three years, she started her own public relations business on the side and accumulated fifty or so clients with whom she works at different times. Sue is a widow and wants to feel more financially comfortable before launching her own business on a full-time basis, which is her goal. While Sue does not quite fall into the Been There, Done That category, she is a good example of someone who has cautiously planned her next career because of her need to earn enough money. She also falls into the Yearning to Be on Your Own category, and by building her business on a part-time basis while earning a regular paycheck, she is satisfying this need as well.

Most people can use the counsel of an outside expert to help them make tough but meaningful changes in their lives. At forty-three, Alison has worked in the publishing industry her entire career. Not only does she feel worn out from working in the same field for so long, but she also admits that she never has been happy in publishing.

"Although I like business, I'm not really the corporate type," Alison says. "I like to learn about what makes people tick. I don't care about fifteen-million-dollar annual quotas. I focus too much stress and energy on a large entity that does not acknowledge me as a person or recognize my talents as an individual, such as my communication skills, sense of humor, and holistic approach to doing business.

"I want to start my own thing," she explains, "but am so multi-faceted that I don't know how to create one thing, and I don't have the cash to create it. But I'm not giving up!"

What Alison needs to do is focus on some viable career options and develop a financial plan, which will help her overcome the obstacle of not having enough money.

Step 3: Create an Action Plan

Now it's time for you to create a plan with concrete steps that will move you out of your Been There, Done That mode.

Your plan should answer the following questions:

• What are all the career or work paths that interest you and are realistic? While the realism factor may not be obvious if you haven't yet investigated what is required to enter a specific field, you'll still be able to make some guesses about this. You can narrow your list later once you've gathered more information. For now, you may want to focus on the list of jobs and industries you prioritized earlier in this chapter.

• What kind of research must you do to learn more about what is entailed in the work you've deemed interesting? To find the answers to this question, you might network at trade association meetings, set up informational meetings with people who work in the job or industry you're interested in, go on interviews, search the Internet, or visit the reference section of the library. While researching the quantifiable aspects of work, such as salaries and educational requirements, is important, the best information comes from talking to people who do the kind of work you think you want to do. Create a list of questions that you can ask everyone you meet so that you will be prepared and will remember everything you heard. Having a list will also help you compare the answers you hear to form your own conclusions. Here are some questions you can ask:

How did you get into this industry?

What experience or characteristics do you think I'm lacking?

What are my advantages?

What suggestions do you have for identifying job opportunities?

• What is a pragmatic time line for moving into another career? Many of your decisions about this will depend on the plan that you and your financial adviser create. Without a plan you won't be able to be specific about your time frame for achieving your career goals. Make sure to factor in the time it will take to prepare for and launch your new career. Depending on your situation, this will include such things as getting a degree or certification, conducting a job search, or the legal processes involved with transactions like buying a franchise or a business. Any of these can take six months to several years or more to accomplish. If you have decided that you absolutely cannot change careers for, say, another four years (perhaps you're not really being realistic), you should still put an action plan in place to help you deal with your Been There, Done That symptoms. Your plan may include learning new skills, working toward a new role within your company or industry, or improving your competence in an outside hobby or interest.

Here are some additional steps to creating an effective action plan:

• Create criteria for yourself that will help you decide when and why you might stop exploring a specific career path. Angela sold shoes for a manufacturer from the time she graduated from college. When she was thirty-eight, she started to question how fulfilled she was at her job and "wondered if I could continue to sell shoes to retail stores between Washington and Boston for the next twenty-two years. But what else could I do? My family depends on me to provide forty percent of the income needed to keep our lifestyle going. I explored becoming a teacher, but the study period was too long, and there wasn't enough money in it. I also explored opening my own business as a Kindermusik or Music Together franchisee, but there was already a lot of competition for children's activities in my geographic area, and they could not give me a franchise in the areas I wanted. I looked into opening my own not-for-profit corporation to help educate and empower the needy but decided I would be too much at the mercy of private and public foundations." Although the results were disappointing for Angela, because she had spent time assessing her own needs and desires carefully, it was easier for her to walk away from a possible career option as soon as it became clear that it would not meet her criteria.

• Create a realistic time line for each of the goals in your plan. Since you aren't trying to make a career change tomorrow, don't try to do too much at once or you will feel overwhelmed and probably give up on your search. Perhaps doing one research activity every two weeks would be good for you. On the other hand, since you don't have an immediate sense of urgency, it's very important to set goals to keep you on track, using your goals and deadlines as motivation to keep you going.

• Find someone to confide in and share what you are doing. Ask this person to be your informal coach and to check in with you periodically to find out how you're doing with your plan so that you'll feel accountable to someone other than yourself.

• Keep an open mind to possibilities that may not have occurred to you. Despite all her exploration, Angela, the persistent shoe salesperson, didn't feel any closer to identifying a new career until a client of hers who owned a shoe store passed away suddenly at forty-two. Her client had not planned for a premature death, and his shoe store was the only source of income for his family. His wife did not know how to run the business on her own, so their son quit college to run the store to support the family. Her late client's misfortune was an eye-opener for Angela. "I couldn't believe how a lack of planning could effectively disrupt an entire family's hopes and dreams for the future so thoroughly," she recalls. It was then that Angela realized she could use her desire to help and teach others by pursuing an occupation that could be both personally and financially rewarding. She became a financial adviser for an insurance and financial company—a career path that had never before occurred to her.

• Start scheduling networking and informational meetings to gather information and meet people. In chapter 12 you will learn specific tips on how to network. Networking is one of the most useful business skills you can develop. Start your networking process with people with whom you feel most comfortable. If you don't know anyone in the jobs or fields that interest you, you'll have to find them first. Do this by making a list of ten or fifteen people whom you trust and who seem well connected to diverse groups of people. It doesn't matter what the people you network with do for a living; what matters is whom they know. Everyone knows someone.

· When you are gathering information about an industry, don't speak to just one person who works in the area you've targeted. Ask all those you meet with for the names of two people in their industry whom you might call or e-mail. Meet with half a dozen people who have varying levels of experience (not just senior-level people) so that you can see the complete picture. Ask such questions as the following:

What do you enjoy about your job and your industry?

What do you dislike?

What are the three things you'd recommend I do to get into your field?

What are the dominant skills that you use most frequently in your job?

Who are the players in your industry that I should meet?

Nick was unemployed. Although he had worked in technical support in the telecommunications industry, he had always had a strong interest in real estate and even had some experience managing family property. He decided to investigate what he needed to do to become a property manager in commercial real estate. He started networking to find people in that field with whom he could talk. He set up his first informational meeting with a real estate broker. During their conversation, the broker made the offhand comment that property managers are all in their late twenties and early thirties. Nick, forty-nine, was gripped by a feeling of insecurity when he heard this and immediately stopped networking. Based on one offhand remark, Nick decided that he would never get a job as a real estate property manager because he was too old. If Nick had continued networking, he might have learned that this simply wasn't so—and even if it were, he might eventually meet or be referred to someone who would be in a position to help him pursue his dream. Although your networking should be targeted, you also need lots of people so you can hit the jackpot with the right job opportunity.

Use JibberJobber.com for all the information and names you gather, or you can create an Excel spreadsheet with the names of those with whom you are networking and notes about your meetings with these contacts.

While you are networking with people and gathering information about industries that interest you, be very inquisitive about the future trends that are taking place within those industries. The World Future Society publishes a magazine about trends in the future called *The Futurist*, which covers work, business, and industry trends. If you are not planning to move into your new career for several years, it is important to be aware of the ways that things could change, either positively or negatively.

Once you have gathered enough information to know whether it is realistic for you to plan on moving into a particular career, here are some things you can and should do to maintain your interest in your potential new career and accelerate your success once you actually do make your move:

• Is a specific degree or certification needed or strongly recommended for your new career? If there is, can you begin studying now on a part-time basis?

• Are there skills you will need to strengthen or have never used that you can begin to work on now? If your plan is to open your own business, for example, and you don't have a clue about accounting or sales, why not take some classes at your local college or university?

• Can you arrange to work part-time at night or on weekends in the field you are interested in, either in a barter situation or for a nominal amount of money, so that you can learn?

• During your networking process, have you met someone who would be a good mentor or coach for you? Many people are flattered to be asked to be a mentor, especially if their investment of time won't be too significant. This is a great way to start learning about a new business.

You may not be able to eliminate or even diminish your financial obligations right now, but you are still in control of planning for your future and, most important, of ending your Been There, Done That blues.

CHAPTER 7

Bruised and Gun-shy

It will come as no great revelation to you that working is difficult. Whether you have always worked for large corporations or for a mix of small- and medium-size privately held companies, you probably have a horror story to tell about a specific job situation. If you have been laid off, discriminated against, or had to deal with a psychotic boss, you are affected adversely both while you're involved in the situation and after you leave, whether or not you realize it. Not only can your negative experience color your outlook about new work opportunities, but it can also prevent you from moving forward in your job search or career when you really need to.

Carol Sommerfield, PhD, counsels many people in her practice who are suffering from psychological abuse in the workplace. "So many clients arrive on my doorstep broken, with their confidence in pieces on the floor," she explains. "They have been emotionally, and often physically, destroyed by working conditions that sound more like the nineteenth century than the twenty-first."

While it is extremely important to deal with what has happened to you and put it into perspective, it is equally important to move on and to identify and engage in the type of work situation that is best for you. This chapter is for you if you can relate to Dr. Sommerfield's clients. You need to recover, and you need to work.

Representative of Dr. Sommerfield's clients, Germaine has worked in a wide range of recruiting and human resources positions and truly feels as if she has had many great jobs, while also experiencing some of the bumps most people experience during their careers. At one point Germaine was diagnosed with breast cancer and, around the same time, was laid off from a great job; a few years later, her mom died; and most recently, her uncle passed away. On top of this, she was hired in a contract recruiting job working remotely, but after four months, the company decided that they didn't need a full-time recruiter. Fortunately, Germaine has been working on the HR benefits side of a large retailer. By doing this part-time for several years and enhancing her skills volunteering for various cancer organizations and attending professional association meetings, she is achieving her personal goals. She balances every penny she spends and gets by; and her ultimate goal is returning to HR full-time.

With several years of college education, Germaine recently started studying for an HR certification that she plans to complete soon. While anyone who knows her would say that she is confident and results-oriented, she confesses to falling squarely into the Bruised and Gun-shy category. At her age, Germaine feels battered by the many situations she has experienced. However, she also knows that it is important to set goals, keep learning, stay marketable, and remove herself from the psychological state she is currently in. She has lived in Seattle for many years, and her goal is to work internationally.

It is not surprising to discover that people aren't very comfortable admitting that they feel Bruised and Gun-shy. Perhaps they feel it isn't professionally appropriate to admit that a negative experience has affected them adversely or that they might be viewed as "damaged goods." Whatever someone's reasons are for not admitting that they were defeated by their specific work experience, the fact remains that at one point or another it happens to most of us. The important thing is to be able to deal with your emotions and feelings about what happened to you. Until you do this effectively, it will be tough to move on.

Suzanne, an administrator in the nonprofit sector, was terminated—unfairly, she thought—because she did not have a master's degree, and the executive director said she needed one. She was upset not only because she loved her job but also because she felt she excelled at it. She also thought that age discrimination was at play in the executive director's decision to fire her. It took more than a year for Suzanne to recover. Her assessment of the workplace today? "It is complicated, to say the least! We have a workforce where mediocrity is the rule. Loyalty is practically nonexistent. Moreover, youth means everything even though experience may be lacking. Workers over the age of forty-five are not desirable, nor, in many cases, are they respected by coworkers and managers. Things are not changing on that front in spite of what's being said by the media. I and others I've met have personally experienced situations where concern about upsetting the chemistry of a team is of the greatest concern—not what you know or how you may help—especially when the team members are between twenty-five and thirty-four. I'm fifty-five—need I say more?"

While age discrimination was Suzanne's issue, feeling Bruised and Gun-shy can happen at any age or time in your career. Jillian was laid off from her first job out of college at a television station because her boss, the director of research, was forced into early retirement. So Jillian's position as her assistant also became extinct. She was then fired from her next job at a radio station because her computer skills weren't up to snuff. At the tender age of twenty-three, Jillian was Bruised and Gun-shy. Her college degree was in broadcasting, and it had never occurred to her that she would do anything else for a living. The thought of finding yet another job in a field where Jillian felt she was "not a very good fit" was not appealing. Her next job after the radio station was as a contingency recruiter for an employment agency. It was the beginning of a long and happy career in sales for Jillian.

Resources and support are important—and available—to help you deal with your emotional state about your painful work situation. Seeing a counselor or therapist can help you understand and sort out your emotions much more quickly than trying to do it on your own.

Suzanne, now happily employed as a copy editor for a small

publishing company where she is using many of the skills she used in nonprofit, also has some sage advice for others that she followed successfully herself: "Don't be too hard on yourself. Give yourself time to heal and don't carry the experience around with you. Move on! Spend some time being good to yourself. Getting terminated from a job happens to others every day, and it has not been known to kill anyone yet." She adds, "Remember, it's not always about you! Sometimes it's about your manager or something completely nonsensical that has nothing to do with the quality of your work or reality! And if you feel as if you have been illegally dismissed or discriminated against, contact the Department of Labor for advice." The US Department of Labor, which has a division that deals with these issues specifically, will answer your questions and determine whether intervention is an appropriate next step. They will also write letters on your behalf.

Many of Carol Sommerfield's clients are referred to her by psychologists who work with them on the psychological aftershock of toxic work environments. Once they become less fragile, they begin the journey to create a positive and healthy career future. As a MBTI (Myers-Briggs Type Indicator) master certified practitioner, Carol Sommerfield focuses on the specific stressors, stress responses, and stress-reduction techniques that are specific to her clients' MBTI personality types to help them understand how they are wired, why they react the way they do, and how to start building their confidence again. Sommerfield says that using this assessment helps validate and affirm people's experiences and explain why one person finds a work situation intolerable while another shrugs it off.

Now it's time to evaluate how your difficult work experiences have impacted you negatively and the actions you can take to pull yourself out of this work situation by following this three-step process.

Step 1: Complete the "Bruised and Gun-shy" Self-Assessments

A recurring theme and recommended first step in this book is to know yourself first before you reach out to the external world. If you know your preferences, your values, and your parameters, you will find it easier to understand your needs and boundaries in a work situation. For example, if stability, security, affiliation, and a regular paycheck are important to you, starting a business or working as a freelancer may not be the best choices for you to pursue. First, review the results of the values, attitudes, and change resilience self-assessments you completed earlier in chapter 3, on pages 33, 35–36, and 41. By doing this you will have a better chance of identifying the best job for you and avoiding another unpleasant work situation.

It makes sense to reflect on your past work situation to help you assess what you'll need and want in your future work. Using the results of the self-assessments you just reviewed, think about the specific work situation that was difficult or painful for you and answer the following questions.

VALUES

Were my values truly being met in that particular work situation?

_____

_____

Which ones were?

_____

_____

_____

Which values were not?

_____

_____

_____

ATTITUDES

Look back at the job or work situation that caused you to feel Bruised and Gun-shy and assess what you have learned about your attitudes.

_____

_____

_____

_____

_____

_____

SELF-CONFIDENCE

Has your self-confidence eroded? If it has, focus on using one of your strengths or skills to help regain your confidence.

If you are working now, is there a task or project you can complete or a goal you can reach that will help you feel good about yourself as well as give you recognition? If you aren't working currently, can you find a freelance or consulting project in which you can use your technical expertise to help a client solve a problem? Write down your ideas.

_____

_____

_____

_____

SELF-KNOWLEDGE

Did you learn something new about yourself during your difficult situation that you were not aware of previously? Did you receive feedback about a specific behavior or skill? Be honest with yourself.

Write down what it is along with three ways that you can change or improve it (take a class, identify a mentor, buy a self-help e-book).

_____

_____

_____

MANAGING RELATIONSHIPS

Did you experience friction or discord with a specific person during your difficult work experience? While some people are truly tough to deal with in the workplace, a relationship involves two people, not just one. What did you learn from your negative experience about the way you handle relationships? If you became involved in a difficult relationship at work again, what would you do differently?

_____

_____

_____

MAINTAINING MOTIVATION

Do you feel focused and energetic about your career? Does the work you've been involved with still interest and stimulate you? If not, write down three to five activities that you can become involved with that would increase your motivation overall. Some suggestions are increasing your exercise routine, taking an art class, researching a new industry, and volunteering for a social cause.

_____

_____

GOAL ORIENTATION

Setting goals is an important part of making changes. Regardless of how severe your Bruised and Gun-shy state is, you must set goals for yourself and your career. Write down two goals that will help you move toward a more optimistic frame of mind. Examples: Completing all the assessments in this book and spending two hours a week researching a new career.

PROFESSIONAL COMMITMENT

Do you feel completely committed to your job and your career? If not, is it because you feel battered by your recent negative work experience or because you no longer have passion for or interest in your career? Write down the things you can do to regain the professional commitment you once had.

CHANGE RESILIENCE

Refer to the results of your self-assessment on handling change on pages 41–42. If you are Bruised and Gun-shy, it is likely your score will reflect this by indicating that you are not comfortable making changes. Identify two positive changes related to work that you can make today or tomorrow that will help you move away from being Bruised and Gun-shy.

_____

_____

_____

INTERESTS

When you think about the work situation that left you feeling Bruised and Gun-shy, how did you feel about the actual work itself? Was the work interesting to you? If so, what about the work interested you/was interesting to you?

_____

_____

_____

Were there aspects of your job that did not interest you? If so, what were they? Describe why they did not interest you.

_____

_____

_____

Step 2: Explore Roadblocks and Opportunities

Once you have determined that you are healing and are more equipped to decide what kind of work situation is right for you, it is time to prepare yourself in case you inadvertently walk into another difficult situation. While this may seem to be a negative approach, the truth is that the likelihood of your being laid off, caught in a merger, or accepting a job with a company whose culture isn't a fit for you is very strong. Even if you decide to start your own business or work as a contractor, there is no guarantee that you will experience success. You are human, after all, and many forces affect your work that you cannot control.

Rupert, a general manager in consumer products, has had a successful career but has had several very difficult patches along the way. While he does admit to being Bruised and Gun-shy, he also says that he has learned how to deal with arduous times in his career that he knows will occur again. In his last position he worked for someone who admitted to Rupert in his first interview that his nickname was the "Yale Terminator." Unfortunately, Rupert ignored this obvious sign that his prospective boss was cruel and took the job anyway because it was a challenging international opportunity. When he left his position, he said that he felt he was in physical danger from his boss. What is Rupert's advice? "Separate what was about you and what was about the other person. Hang on to the fundamental realization that nothing will last forever. Take the position and the work for what it's worth. No matter what you were promised when you were hired, accept it because that's as good as it gets. Manage your expectations." He adds, "You lose a certain elasticity as you move along in your career, and you need to have something to fall back on. Have a support group. For me it's my wife and my kids."

Usually, when people interview for a new job, they look at the job title, location, work responsibilities, and compensation first. Although these factors are important, they are rarely the reason that a job doesn't work out. Instead, the primary reason may be your boss, the company culture, or the job was misrepresented or changed once you were in it. You can help avoid these problems by doing the following before you accept a new job.

1. Assess Your Prospective Boss

Bill DeLeno, a psychotherapist in private practice in White Plains, New York, specializes in helping people with problems at work. He asserts that the number one difficulty people have at work is their boss. One of Bill's patients actually told him he was so afraid of his boss that he couldn't go to his mother's funeral because he had to work.

Not everyone is as obvious as Rupert's new boss, who admitted up front to Rupert what his horrifying nickname was. If you have had a bad experience with a boss, then you will naturally try to learn as much as you can about the person you'll report to in your next job. Even so, few people feel comfortable "interviewing" their possible future boss. Instead, we behave as if the relationship goes one way rather than two. It is important to keep in mind that this person is crucial to your success or failure in your job, so the more you can find out about your prospective new boss before you start working for him or her, the better off you'll be. Remember that bosses usually show their "best face" to you during the interviewing process, especially if they see you as a viable candidate for the job they are trying to fill. If your prospective boss is rude, insensitive, or appears uninterested in you during the interview, this behavior will only become magnified during your working relationship. Asking the following questions will help uncover his or her personality quirks and style:

How would you describe the ideal relationship you could have with someone who reports to you?

What would you expect of me during my first three months at this job? First six months? First year?

How does this align with the organization's expectations?

What about its strategy?

What about your job keeps you up at night? How would I help you with the solution to this challenge?

How do you like to communicate and receive information from the people who report to you? How often?

How would you describe your work style?

What should I realistically expect from you as my manager? Who was the best boss you ever had and why?

What are your top three values?

How do you think people view you within the organization?

Some of these are tough questions to ask; however, an individual's willingness to answer the questions and his or her candor in doing so can be very telling. When you ask any or all of these questions, do so in a nonthreatening way so that your prospective boss isn't turned off.

The most useful information you can get about your prospective boss is from the people who presently work for him or her or have done so in the past. Why is it okay for the people interviewing you to ask you whatever they are legally allowed to and it isn't okay for you? It's not right! Working involves a mutual agreement. Your response to the question "Why do you want to talk with these people?" is the following: "I want a productive relationship that is going to be the best possible fit for both of us. I know what it costs to recruit, hire, and retain an employee, financially and psychologically."

Whoever you question may be cautious about answering, particularly when the answers may not be positive. Again, be sensitive to their position of needing to protect themselves and their job. Read between the lines and probe.

Scott wishes he had been more thorough about this before he accepted his last job as Chief Marketing Officer/Executive Vice President of Sales with a start-up technology company. His boss, who was the owner, was a trained lawyer who had never run a business before he bought the small software company. Though Scott was a member of the executive team, his boss would unilaterally make major decisions, such as choosing vendors or moving in new business directions. There was no formal internal communication with employees, including performance reviews, and to top it off, Scott's boss would have emotional outbursts over minor snafus. While the company was well funded, won prestigious awards, and was recognized in the industry, the product didn't sell well, which resulted in Scott's boss becoming even more erratic. Scott left because of poor business results and admits that even if the company was hitting its goals, he would have found another job because he couldn't deal with the owner's behavior any longer.

When you are speaking to someone who currently works for or has reported in the past to your prospective boss, ask these questions:

How would you describe your relationship with him or her?

What are his or her strengths? What are areas that may need development?

How is he or she viewed within the organization? Why?

Who is he or she close to in the organization?

Does he or she make decisions? Does he or she involve you in those decisions?

How does he or she like to communicate (regular meetings, in the hallway, e-mail, reports, voice mail)?

How would you describe his or her work style?

Does he or she give feedback? How and when?

What characteristics does he or she admire?

Does he or she value and support work-life balance?

How does he or she deal with conflict?

What are his or her priorities in his or her job?

What are his or her hot buttons or pet peeves?

If he or she hires me, what advice would you give me to ensure that he or she and I get started on the right foot?

You will notice that some of these questions are the same as the ones you've asked your prospective boss. Pay attention to which of the answers are the same or similar and which are not.

If your prospective boss is new to the organization, ask him if you can speak to someone at his previous job. Again, if he balks, be concerned.

With the constant change that occurs within organizations, you may not be working for the same person for very long. We all know, however, that even three months of working for someone with whom we don't get along can feel like an eternity!

2. Assess the Company's Culture

Every work environment has its own culture. If you fit into a company's culture—the values employees share, the way people communicate and dress, the behaviors that are accepted—then you probably will have a good working experience. On the other hand, if you don't fit in, regardless of how talented you are at your job or what you've accomplished, the chances are strong that you will either derail voluntarily or be asked to leave the organization.

A company's culture is very powerful and cannot be changed overnight by one person, even a new leader. A culture is an interwoven system of beliefs, values, history, mythology, rituals, and ceremonies. In a work context, these create meaning for people, and although it may not always be easy to describe it to others outside the organization, the company culture definitely influences behavior and the way business is conducted.

Because of this, it is important that you learn how to effectively assess a company's culture to determine if it is a fit for you. Remember, you spend a lot of time working. There is no reason to be unhappy or to be working in an unsuitable work situation. If you have already had an experience in which you went to work for a company and realized you didn't fit into the culture, you know how painful this can be. Learning how to identify the right culture for you is easy to do if you ask the right questions and rely on your intuition.

Jason enjoyed a thirty-year career in IT with a chemical company; then the company was acquired, and he was laid off—which he expected. During his transition, with the help of a government grant, he pursued a career in the health-care industry and landed at a huge health-care company. Although he was elated that he was successful at moving into a different industry in a job that was close to home, Jason quickly realized that his new employer's corporate culture was challenging in many ways, including being extremely impersonal. Human resources and other corporate-support functions were provided primarily through Web sites and mechanical processes. A call for help would take two days for a response, and it was rare to speak with the same person twice. Heavy workloads resulted in sixty- to seventy-hour workweeks until a breaking point was reached, and then work would fall behind when people cut back on the long hours. Throughout the company, people focused on their own agendas and escalated problems, competing for attention. There was steady turnover in staff and management, and the workload piled up and was repeatedly reshuffled.

Jason's friends and family could see that he was miserable. He needed to consider quitting his job, and his financial planner helped him stage some options. The distress from work and consideration of quitting led to anxiety attacks, trouble sleeping, and waking up in a cold sweat. Jason's doctors encouraged him to take a leave of absence, which he did for two months. Toward the end of his leave, Jason notified his boss that he wasn't coming back to his job. Ten months later, he feels more like himself, but he still feels Bruised and Gun-shy about his experience.

Several elements of company culture are important to consider when you are pursuing a new opportunity. One important element is that of values and beliefs. Values and beliefs are principles, standards, or qualities considered inherently worthwhile and desirable. They cannot always be neatly defined in a manual. Values create focus and shape behavior. A historic person in the company (a past leader or pioneer) exemplifies core values and beliefs.

Now that you have identified your own top ten values, it will be easier to ask questions in an interview to find out how closely your values match those of your prospective employer.

Think about what you want in a company culture from a "clean slate" perspective, especially if you have never felt as if you fit into a company culture in the past or have had some disappointments. Sit at your computer or take a piece of paper and list the ideal elements that you want and need to feel comfortable in your work environment. Forget about reality for the moment. You can go back to your list later and focus on what you think is realistic.

How do you assess a company's culture? You do it by asking lots of questions; meeting as many people as you can; sitting in the parking lot and observing; sitting in the reception area; looking at the company's Web site, marketing materials, and annual report; and—*most important*—by following your intuition. As a prospective employee you have every right to talk to as many people as you need to, including vendors, clients, and employees who don't work in your functional area. If there is resistance to this, take note and be wary. Remember, if your gut is telling you that something is not quite right, in all likelihood it isn't! It is okay to be excited or interested in a particular job opportunity, but don't fixate on the title, money, perks, or job description and lose sight of the one aspect of the job that can make or break your chances of success: the culture!

At the same time here is a word of caution: "Fit" means the most suitable. You will not find perfection in any job or work situation, because it does not exist. Companies are not always completely candid about their cultures. This is another reason to try to talk with as many different people as possible before signing on.

Here are some questions you can ask to assess a company's culture:

How would you describe the culture here?

What is important to senior management here?

How are decisions made? (It could be by senior management only, by consensus, collaboratively, by crisis, or not at all.)

What is the typical background of the people here?

How important is the customer or client?

What kind of hierarchy exists in the company?

What is the preferred method of communication (e-mail, memos, meetings, voice mail, or impromptu hallway conversations)?

Is feedback valued? Does it occur and in what form?

Is innovation or risk taking valued and rewarded?

How often, when, and why do people leave the company? (Is it of their own volition or are people fired?)

Who are some of the successful people in the company, and why are they successful?

Psychotherapist Bill DeLeno advises that even if you've done a thorough job of assessing a company, "you don't know what you've got until you get there." While it's not easy advice to follow, Bill recommends that if you do find yourself in a situation that is making you very unhappy and you can't seem to change it, "don't linger if it's bad. Every job and work experience is a stepping-stone today anyway."

3. Assess the Job Itself

When you are interviewing for a new job, it is normal to ask questions about the responsibilities you'll have. It is also important to ask questions about the business goals you'll be expected to achieve. Whether you are starting a new job with a company or moving into a new role with your current employer, ask these questions of your boss:

Why does this job exist?

What are your expectations of me in my first three months in this position?

How will you measure my success after a year in this job?

How does this job fit within the department or division?

Who worked in this job before, and where did he or she go?

What did he or she accomplish in this job?

What was difficult for him or her?

What do you think my greatest challenge will be in this job?

What are the three most important business priorities in this job?

Whenever you start a new job or are promoted, create a plan with your new boss and any other stakeholders (which include peers, direct reports, and senior management) who can influence your work and job.

Jackie received a big promotion to run operations for the sales division of her company. Jackie was an assistant controller with no experience in sales. When she was asked what her plans were for her first thirty, sixty, and ninety days, she didn't even have a plan. It hadn't even occurred to her. Not only did she need to understand what her boss was interested in accomplishing, but she was also inheriting a big staff. The first thing she should have done was make an appointment with her new boss and prepare a list of questions for him. She then should have scheduled a one-on-one meeting with every person on her staff to get to know them individually and understand what they had contributed in the past as well as what they would like to do moving forward. Jackie needed to make a strong first impression on everyone in her new role because the department was experiencing problems and because initially Jackie wouldn't have seemed an obvious choice for the job.

Once Jackie gathered all this information and started to develop relationships, she needed to set goals that were measurable and realistic, and have her boss and other stakeholders sign off on them. Going forward, Jackie should meet with everyone at least every forty-five to sixty days. If possible, she should make an ally out of the person who was previously in her role.

It is just as important to continue assessing your job once you've been doing it for a while. While most people who are laid off from their jobs aren't fired because of performance, people do lose their jobs because business priorities shift. With this shift comes the assumption that different skills may be needed. Most companies aren't very good at assessing their employees' skills and putting them in a different role that will benefit both employees and their company. Often a person is hired to accomplish one thing, and if the needs of the organization change, that person may no longer be viewed as relevant to the company's new priorities. Sometimes it is difficult to know whether you are still viewed as integral to the company's priorities. How can you be aware of this in your company so that you are not caught off guard? Unfortunately, very few people are aware that they may be losing their job before they actually do. Sadly, not many people take care of the things that they can control before they lose their job. As a result, the recovery period takes much longer.

What can you do to stay aware of the status of your job? Pay attention to specific signs, such as budget cuts, positions that remain unfilled, not being invited to meetings you used to attend, or your boss suddenly being too busy to meet with you. Instead of burying your head in the sand in an effort to avoid what might be happening, consider trying practical activities that will help you to feel more prepared if you do end up losing your job. Here are some recommendations:

Update your résumé and LinkedIn profile.

Start networking with recruiters, your competition, former colleagues, and trade associations.

Get organized by cleaning out your desk and computer files and backing them up.

Use your benefits by scheduling all those doctors' appointments you've been putting off. Staying healthy is even more important when you're going through this stressful time.

Simplify your life by reducing clutter and winnowing down scheduled activities.

Reorganize your finances by assessing your savings and looking at areas where you can cut expenses, and avoid using credit cards.

Take a class to refresh or learn a business skill that is relevant to your professional area of focus.

Taking action in these areas will help you feel more in control and less stressed in the event that you do lose your job.

Step 3: Create an Action Plan

Now that you've looked at what you learned from your past work experiences and determined what you want from your next job, it is important to create a plan to move ahead.

Answer the following questions:

What do you want your work to look like in three months? Six months? A year? Describe it as specifically as you can.

Three months

_____

_____

_____

Six months

_____

_____

_____

A year

_____

_____

_____

What steps do you need to take to make this happen? What kind of research should you do? What resources do you need to move forward?

Steps to take (for example, update your résumé and LinkedIn profile, set up meetings with people in your network, and have a conversation with your current boss):

_____

_____

Research to do (for example, learn about a new industry, interview several people who are working in a job that you'd like to do):

_____

_____

_____

Resources you need (for example, buy a new computer, find a mentor):

_____

_____

_____

_____

Do you want to be on your own? If this is the route you think you'd like to take, it is even more important to recover from feeling Bruised and Gun-shy because planning and starting a new business will tap all your energy and many of your resources.

Pat was a managing counsel for a major commercial bank. She had a great job but had been doing it for twenty years. She stayed because she liked the work and it was near her home and two children. But then the bank began to sell off assets in her area. Pat was laid off two weeks before she turned fifty. "I was traumatized at first and started looking for a job with another large financial company, although everyone told me that I should be in my own business. I took some private clients during my job search. I loved it and decided to go into business for myself. That's a very risky thing to do at my age, since I need to maintain a certain income level and my husband is not making a lot. But it has turned out to be a very rewarding second career."

If you want to follow Pat's lead, ask yourself the following questions:

If you want to be on your own, what kind of work do you want to do?

_____

_____

_____

_____

How will you begin the process of planning your own business? (Read chapter 9, "Yearning to Be on Your Own," first!)

_____

_____

_____

How will you manage stress and maintain your psychological well-being (for example, take yoga classes, start a blog, spend extra time with your family)?

_____

_____

Before she was fired, Susie worked in sales. Her employer and another larger company merged, and she was let go for "political" reasons. "I stayed a year longer than I should have," Susie admits, "because I was determined to make it work." Her counsel to others? "Remember who you are. Remember what successes you've had in the past. Don't let anyone strip away your self-confidence. Stay whole."

List three successes you've had in your career that you are especially proud of:

_____

_____

Patty Forbes, LCSW, has been counseling people in her private practice in New York City since 2002. Before Patty became a therapist, she went through her own career transition. For years, she worked in the commercial music business as a sales and marketing rep and as a jingle singer. While she enjoyed the creative element, she hated the need to sell on a constant basis. When Patty decided she wanted to be a therapist, she had to start from scratch—earning her bachelor's and master's degrees and then completing a requisite three years of postgraduate hours. Having successfully changed careers herself, she can relate to clients who are in difficult work situations.

Patty's advice to clients who have been traumatized by being fired or laid off or who have worked for a company with a difficult or "toxic" culture is to "try to change your perspective. Assigning a 'negative' to choice is inhibiting and paralyzing."

She explains that the negative work situation can provide an opportunity to make new choices. She encourages her clients to assess what their actual fear is, whether it is making "another" wrong move, losing status and being judged by others, or simply dreading the unknown. She refers to these types of life challenges as "the gifts in the black box." Then she helps her clients examine their resiliency and identify the areas of their lives where they have been successful and where they haven't. Once they realize that they have achieved goals and been happy in other aspects of their lives, Patty encourages them to remember what they did to be successful and to take a similar approach with work.

Patty often says to her clients, "You are not sentenced to a job with no parole. You can leave a job whenever you want." She adds, "Life is a series of rule-outs, and you should have lots of life experiences; this is how we learn about ourselves."

Whatever your current and future work choices are for yourself—staying in your present job, changing careers, starting a business, or retiring—think of what you've learned from the difficult working situations you have experienced. Use these lessons to be more prepared to deal with losing your job, working for a difficult boss, or experiencing a merger. While much of what has happened to you in the past may have been out of your control, if you are clear about what you need and can tolerate in your next work situation, you will feel more in control should you get involved in another difficult situation.

CHAPTER 8

Bored and Plateaued

Most of us have felt bored or unchallenged at some point in our lives, whether for a few hours, several months, or even years at a time. If you have been involved in the same kind of work for a while, you've probably reached the top of your game from a competency standpoint. It feels good to be viewed by your professional peers, friends, and family as an expert in your field. Chances are you also enjoy many perks, including healthy compensation, status, and the overall feeling of having "made it" in your career.

But the picture might not be completely rosy. You may be so comfortable that you have begun to feel plateaued, which is to say stifled, unchallenged, or bored. Not only do you feel listless, restless, aimless, or disengaged with the tasks you are performing or the people you work with, but you also exhibit "bored" behaviors. These behaviors may include texting your friends, watching cat videos on YouTube, using Reddit or Instagram, taking at least half a dozen coffee and food breaks, and fantasizing about becoming the next fifty-million-dollar Powerball lottery winner and telling your boss that you're quitting your job. When you're bored and your coworkers don't seem to be bored, you naturally feel alienated and weird.

Feeling Bored or Plateaued can occur gradually so that you are able to shrug it off for a time, or it may come on suddenly and linger chronically so that it isn't quite as easy to ignore. If you are feeling bored, you may not necessarily be feeling plateaued. If you are experiencing one of these feelings, however, you are probably susceptible to the other as well.

Being Bored or Plateaued does not mean that you aren't working hard or that you don't have enough work to do. Being busy and dealing with the excessive stimulation that the workplace provides us with today have little to do with being bored. The combination of the two merely leads to a greater level of burnout.

Dr. Jack Zenger and Dr. Joe Folkman of Zenger|Folkman, a respected global leadership development training company, coined the phrase "day prison" to describe the phase in which many people find themselves when they feel that work is a chore, a common symptom of being bored. To better understand the phenomenon, they examined data from 970 people in the same organization who were between thirty-five and forty-four years old and who rated their engagement at work in the bottom 10 percent. They declared themselves in "day prison." Zenger and Folkman identified eight distinctive themes that characterized the frustration of these employees, and one of them was the absence of challenge and meaning in their work. Some jobs are challenging at first, but after ten thousand iterations of doing the same things over and over again, it is easy for this to become monotonous and boring.

Just like boredom, feeling plateaued can catch many people by surprise. When you were promoted in the past, you knew that with that promotion would come new experiences, different relationships, and the opportunity to develop additional skills. If you have been in the same job for several years or haven't learned anything new for a while, it is easy to become stifled by repetition and disinterested in the overfamiliar tasks you routinely perform. Although it is normal for a productive person to experience such feelings on occasion, there are many negative ramifications of being in this predicament, particularly long-term. For one thing, it becomes increasingly difficult to hide your feelings from your boss, peers, subordinates, and clients. Rachelle, a senior human resources director, recalls being pulled aside by her boss and asked if she wanted to take some extended time off because she didn't seem engaged in her work the way she used to be. She expressed surprise that her boss had picked up on her boredom so easily.

If you have been in the same job for a while, without the benefit of ongoing continuing education opportunities, your skills may become outdated and you could be viewed by others as someone who is no longer current. Research has shown over and over again, that the healthiest, most productive adult is the one who is constantly learning and growing, not the one who is stagnant.

Working in a job or career where you are Bored and Plateaued can produce many negative emotional, psychological, and physical effects. Feeling depressed, anxious, unmotivated, or frustrated not only impacts your work but also the rest of your life, including your significant relationships and even your health.

Andie worked for ten years in finance as a fixed income analyst after graduating from college with a degree in engineering. She found herself feeling more and more dissatisfied with the repetition of her work, as well as feeling that her values were not aligned with the values of her employer's corporate culture. However, Andie truly had no idea what she wanted to do—or even could do—workwise to be happy. Her whole life, her parents had dictated to her what she should and shouldn't do, never asking her what she was interested in.

Andie started feeling depressed and also experienced a number of seemingly random injuries, such as a blood clot, bursitis, pink eye, and a torn ACL that seemed to be stress-related. Feeling that she was at the end of her rope, Andie decided to see a therapist who began giving her writing assignments as a method for expressing her interests and needs. When the therapist read her work, she recognized that Andie had real talent as a writer and encouraged her to take a graduate-level writing class. Andie's therapist then suggested that she apply to graduate school, so Andie applied to and was accepted by Columbia University's Journalism School in New

York City on a part-time basis. A week after Andie was accepted, she was laid off from her job as senior director at a large financial services company. Andie was relieved as she realized that her boredom at work had negatively impacted her entire life and she has vowed to never let this happen again.

If you like your field or aspects of the work you do but have mastered the essentials and are hungry to learn new things, you are probably Bored and Plateaued. It is time to learn what you can do to change your feelings from Bored and Plateaued to committed, creative, competent, and energized. Remember also that many people feel bored or stifled at some point in their career, so it's important to analyze your situation carefully and identify the culprit—what is really boring you—before taking action to eliminate those feelings.

Step 1: Complete the "Bored and Plateaued" Self-Assessment

Flip back to the self-assessments you took on interests on pages 49–55 and favorite skills on pages 56–60. Review your responses.

Now it's time to look at your current work situation. Answer these questions. Your goal is to identify your interests and favorite skills that are being satisfied in your job currently and to think of ways to eliminate some of the things that are causing you to feel Bored and Plateaued.

1. How would you describe what you do for a living? Avoid using a title of any kind.

_____

_____

_____

_____

2. Which of your favorite skills do you use most frequently in your current position? (Refer to your list of favorite skills in chapter 4.)

_____

_____

3. What do you like the most about your job (tangible or intangible)?

_____

_____

_____

_____

4. How could you augment this aspect of your job? Be specific.

_____

_____

_____

_____

5. What do you like least about your job (tangible or intangible)?

_____

_____

_____

_____

6. Can you find a way to reduce or eliminate this aspect? If so, describe how.

_____

_____

_____

_____

7. Describe your feelings of boredom.

_____

_____

_____

_____

8. Describe why you feel plateaued.

_____

_____

_____

_____

9. Do you currently have any specific career goals? If so, what are they?

_____

_____

_____

10. What do you believe are the obstacles preventing you from moving out of your Bored and Plateaued situation?

_____

_____

_____

_____

11. What could help you move into a fulfilling and rewarding work situation?

_____

_____

_____

_____

Answering these basic questions should help you understand your current work situation more clearly. You will refer to your answers later.

Step 2: Explore Roadblocks and Opportunities

Deb was a forty-year-old vice president of marketing in the consumer products industry who was "bored silly" and felt stuck in her job. She was unchallenged and not using her strengths, and because she had been in this Bored and Plateaued phase for several years, she was not motivated to make a career change though she desperately wanted to. Deb dreamed of being an interior designer or working in the fashion industry.

When Deb finally began to do something about her feelings, she took a series of assessments. They revealed that she is extroverted, intuitive, makes decisions based on her values, and prefers spontaneity. Her primary values are creativity and autonomy. A typical baby boomer, she was concerned about earning less money than she previously earned, and because she hadn't saved much, she wasn't willing to decrease her compensation dramatically. She is single, and although she works hard when challenged, she was very interested in attaining a balanced lifestyle. Since she estimated that she would have to work for another twenty-five years, Deb wanted to move into a field that offers a variety of opportunities for her to work flexibly and long-term.

When Deb answered the questions listed on pages 129–132, she discovered the chances were slim that she would ever muster the interest or energy to change something about her current job to alleviate her boredom. The truth is that although she knew her business well and was very comfortable, she just couldn't bring herself to think of ways to revitalize her situation to make it work for her. She yearned to leave consumer products marketing. Fortunately, she knew that she was interested in the interior design and fashion fields. She was also pretty clear about what her skills were—in the areas of marketing, operations, and working with clients. Because she was certain that just changing her current situation wouldn't alleviate her boredom and that she wanted to move out of her field altogether, she was faced with the prospect of changing careers. Deb's first obstacle was believing that it was actually possible for her to switch fields without taking a significant cut in pay. She was especially worried about having to accept an entry-level position with an entry-level salary. Initially, this fear slowed her down. Like many prospective career changers, Deb put obstacles in her own way to mask her fear of the unknown. In his book *The Pathfinder*, Nicholas Lore calls these manufactured obstacles "Yeahbuts." He lists twenty-five or so, including "I don't have enough talent," "I'm too young/too stupid," "I'm not committed enough," "I'm over-/undereducated," "I'm over-/underqualified," and "I have too much/too little experience."

Yet once Deb had made up her mind that changing fields was what she was going to do, her entire attitude shifted and she felt excited about her next career. She began brainstorming ways to meet people in the interior design and fashion industries so that she could learn more about the kinds of opportunities that might exist for her. Deb started networking with people in her two target industries. She didn't spend a lot of time doing it, but every week she would talk on the phone or meet with someone in interior design or fashion. As she became immersed in this process, her excitement grew, confirming that she was correct in her original assessment: She should be working in fashion or interior design. Interestingly, once Deb found the motivation to change careers, she wasn't nearly as focused on the issue of compensation.

Every once in a while Deb's energy flagged, and she would stop networking. When this happened, she would identify one simple action step to reignite the spark, which would help her feel motivated once again. Then, after three months, Deb ran into Ursula, a friend from high school, and as she did with everyone, she told her what she was trying to do. Her friend reminded Deb that another mutual friend, Cynthia, whom Deb hadn't seen in a long time, owned an agency for designers in New York City. Deb met with Cynthia, who gave her several names of people to contact in the design industry. Deb started calling them. Not long afterward she heard from Cynthia, who asked if she would be interested in running sales for her business, since the person in that position was going on maternity leave and not planning to return. Deb jumped at the opportunity and worked for Cynthia for nearly two years. Once she learned about the business, she took a leap and started an interior design firm with a partner and, eight years later, has never experienced a bored moment!

Deb is an example of someone who changed her Bored and Plateaued status by leaving her job and her industry. The first thing you should do if you are feeling Bored and Plateaued is take a look at your current situation.

Favorite Skills

How did you respond to the question "Which of your favorite skills do you use most frequently in your current position?" Whatever favorite skills you identified, would you feel more engaged and interested if you could increase the time you spent using these? If you like to write but write only business reports and e-mails, is there a way to increase the amount of writing you do by starting a blog or approaching your local newspaper to write a monthly column?

Remember Andie, who was bored with her financial services career? She earned her master's degree in journalism, which she paid for herself, and now enjoys a career as a freelance writer of numerous published articles and white papers as well as a subject matter expert on TV and radio. As she took various graduate classes, she remembered that she used to enjoy writing essays when she was in high school. Andie works very hard and struggles with balancing work and her personal life, but she is adamant that she could never again see herself going to an office every day as an employee. And she is happier than she has ever been and, thankfully, being Bored and Plateaued is a distant memory for Andie.

Take a look at the favorite skills you wrote down on pages 58–59 and think of different opportunities you could create to make them a bigger part of your work life. Write down every possible opportunity you come up with. For the moment forget about any obstacles you perceive that could prevent you from making it happen.

_____

_____

_____

_____

_____

_____

Tasks

Take a look at your list of things you least enjoy in your work from page 130. Doing tasks that we don't enjoy can lead to boredom and ultimately to unhappiness. Put on your creative hat and think of ways to get these tasks off your plate. Is there someone to whom you could delegate them—an intern, assistant, junior staff member, outside vendor, or peer—who enjoys that type of work more than you do? If you could eliminate or reduce these tasks you don't enjoy, and spend your time doing other things, would you be less bored? Write down the list of tasks along with ideas for delegating or eliminating them.

_____

_____

_____

_____

Remember When You Weren't Bored?

Can you think back and recall when you began to feel bored in your work? Did boredom creep up on you slowly, or was it triggered by a specific incident or situation? Write down how you think it would feel if you were no longer bored in your work. If you can't imagine what that would feel like, look back on your career and try to recall a time when you felt energized and challenged. How was your situation then different from the situation you're in now?

_____

_____

_____

_____

Revitalizing Your Current Situation

Despite being Bored and Plateaued, you may decide to stay with your current employer for a year or two more, or you may not. If you're leaning toward leaving your present job, before you do, make sure you have explored what you could change in your current job situation that could alleviate your current state.

How? First, be clear about what you'd like to change before you approach other people in your organization. Also be sure that you are able to communicate what the benefit is to your employer. Let's take Rachelle's situation, mentioned earlier. Rachelle's boss had asked her if she wanted to take time off because she seemed bored and disinterested in her work. Rachelle grabbed the opportunity. After taking three weeks off and traveling, Rachelle realized that she really loved human resources and just needed a new challenge. Although she did begin to conduct a job search outside her company, Rachelle, who loves to travel, ended up interviewing for and accepting a human resources director position for her current employer, in which she provides support for the company's Latin American division. In her new job she works in a function she loves and has more autonomy. She feels energized and stimulated, quite different from the way she felt just six months before she started her new position.

Rachelle is fortunate that she works for a company large enough to provide internal job opportunities for its employees. Her employer realized that Rachelle, a talented HR professional with exceptional people skills and an understanding of the complex political workings of the organization, was an asset to the company and an employee worth keeping.

Even though you may work for a smaller company, if you and your employer are creative, you will find ways to add new and different responsibilities to your current job and prepare an exciting new job description. Most Bored and Plateaued people immediately think about leaving their company rather than finding a way to change their present work situation. But leaving isn't always the answer. If your employer values you, then it is in his or her best interest to keep you and to help you find a way to reenergize yourself, for the benefit of the organization. If not, there is a company out there that *will* appreciate you.

Changing the dynamics of your job may or may not be the solution to your Bored and Plateaued state. Learning something new can be an effective hedge against boredom, but those familiar feelings may return once you've mastered a new skill or successfully taken on a new challenge. That is why it's so critical to analyze the source of your Bored and Plateaued feelings before applying what could turn out to be merely a Band-Aid solution.

Staying in Your Industry

If you have investigated changing your work or moving into a new position at your current company but there are real obstacles to making this happen or you really don't want to change careers right now, there are several other options you can explore. The most obvious is to find a new position in your current industry—either the same type of job you have now or a different role in another company. Be cautious about using this tactic. Consider the case of Donna. She was a human resource generalist for a publishing company. After six years she was bored but decided to "hang in" because of rumors of an impending takeover of her company by another publishing house. Sure enough, this occurred, and Donna received a nice severance package. After taking the summer off, she started her job search. Results from assessments and feedback from several friends helped Donna discover that she had the ideal personality for sales. Although sales sounded appealing to her, the thought of leaving HR and taking a risk made her nervous, so she accepted the first offer she received—as an HR generalist at a relocation company. Unfortunately, it was a bad fit. Donna couldn't relate to the employees and was uncomfortable not only with the way they communicated but also with many other aspects of the company culture. She decided to quit, without having another job, and then worked as a temporary recruiter for six months. Again she conducted a job search and, ignoring the voice in her head and her friends' advice, accepted yet another HR generalist position in the publishing industry. Although this time the firm's culture is comfortable for Donna, she is back where she was almost two years ago. Sitting at her desk, she is still thinking about how to find the courage to leave human resources and go into sales. Unfortunately, Donna is plagued with doubts and keeps hearing the message she received growing up: Find a good job with a decent salary and stick with it through thick and thin.

Dean is another example of someone who is Bored and Plateaued. Having worked in the entertainment industry for ten years, he was bored. At the beginning of each new job (he has had three), he wasn't at all bored because he had to adjust to a different culture, get to know new players, and learn new skills. When he really explored the root of his boredom, however, Dean discovered that throughout his career he had been using many skills that he really wasn't interested in using, and he wasn't using others that he loved. Dean determined that he wanted to write more, develop creative messages or promotional campaigns, and function in a more persuasive role. He also had a deep interest in current affairs, politics, and media. Dean created a list of favorite skills that he wanted to be using every day; he identified public affairs, public relations, and media consulting as avenues to explore. Once he identified these new areas, he felt excited and very committed.

Changing jobs in your industry makes sense if you love the industry and haven't yet accomplished the things you'd like to accomplish or learned everything you could. It also makes sense if you're unable to move into a role that interests you within your current company. If this is what you want, be very focused and adamant about communicating to prospective employers in your industry that you will move only if you are given a role that is different from the one you currently have. Otherwise, it is likely that you'll be bored after six months to a year and be back to where you were before you changed jobs.

Focusing on the World Outside of Work

Another solution to overcoming boredom or lack of learning in your work is to focus your energy on the world outside of your job. As adults we all have interests or untapped talents that we've allowed to fade because of our work and family responsibilities. Take a look at the results of your interests self-assessment (page 54) and select one thing that jumps out at you. Plan to take a class, hire a coach, or attend a workshop. It is not recommended that you ignore your Bored and Plateaued state at work indefinitely, but revitalizing yourself in another area of your life can energize your personal life now and your career later on.

By getting involved in something that you find fun, exciting, interesting, or fulfilling, you may discover the key to ending boredom in your career. You also may learn how to weave your outside interests into your work. This can be accomplished in several ways.

One option is to immerse yourself in your interest outside of work while working your "day job" to satisfy your need to earn a living. Robert is an example. An avid foxhunter who owns two horses, he spends nearly all his spare time either foxhunting or socializing with other foxhunters. During the week, however, he puts on business clothes and drives into Atlanta to his job as a contingency recruiter for an agency. While he doesn't particularly like his job, he earns a good living, which allows him to support his expensive outside interest. This is an easy trade-off for him to make since his enjoyment of foxhunting far outweighs the boredom he feels at his job.

Another option is to do as Julia did: eventually find a way to turn your passion into a full-time job. For eight years, Julia did speaking engagements on such topics as sales, networking, and career management for local associations for free, simply because she enjoyed giving talks. Every year the number of speeches she gave increased. Several years ago, when she was at a crossroad in her sales career, she was having lunch with an acquaintance who commented that Julia lit up when she talked about public speaking. That moment changed Julia's life. Soon after that lunch, she began to make plans to speak professionally. It had never occurred to her that public speaking was what she should do for a living. Until that moment Julia simply thought of it as a fun hobby.

Turning an avocation into a vocation can be a scary proposition; doing it successfully requires planning that includes preparing yourself psychologically and financially. After that fateful lunch, Julia spent eight months working in a transitional job she disliked while planning and priming herself to start her professional speaking practice. As stressful as Julia's "for the time being" job was, the income and structure it offered made her transition much smoother and less frightening.

If you can't shake the feeling that "it just isn't fun anymore," it's time to realize it, accept it, and begin moving forward. Start small by learning something new, or start looking at your job from the outside in and think about how you can approach it differently. Ideas? Take a webinar or a class, get certified in something, research new trends, or pitch in to help another department. And if that doesn't nip your boredom in the bud, start the exhilarating process of changing your career.

Step 3: Create an Action Plan

As you figure out how you intend to eliminate your Bored and Plateaued situation, you need to have clear answers to the following questions.

What are the reasons for your boredom with work?

_____

_____

How can you revitalize or change your current job or working situation so that you won't be bored?

_____

_____

_____

Do you want to pursue a different job within your industry? If so, how will you do this?

_____

_____

_____

What are the reasons that you would accept another job in your industry?

_____

_____

_____

_____

Have you decided to change careers and leave your industry? If so, write down what steps you will take in the following five areas:

Self-assessment

_____

_____

_____

_____

Research

_____

_____

_____

_____

Writing your résumé

_____

_____

_____

_____

Creating or updating your social networking profiles

_____

_____

_____

_____

Networking to learn about the industry you're interested in and to uncover job openings

_____

_____

_____

_____

Do you have a hobby or interest that you'd like to spend more time with? If so, what do you need to do to make this happen?

_____

_____

_____

_____

Regardless of what you decide to do first, it is important that you do something—anything—to begin to alleviate your feeling of boredom. Use your Bored and Plateaued state as a launch pad to new and satisfying work. The choice is yours.

CHAPTER 9

Yearning to Be on Your Own

If you are dreaming of starting your own business, you are not alone. Amway, the world's largest direct selling company, surveyed forty thousand people for their 2014 Amway Global Entrepreneurship Report and found that 75 percent of respondents have positive attitudes toward entrepreneurship, with two out of five or 42 percent saying that they can definitely imagine starting a business. Even more interesting, the majority of respondents—63 percent—reported that they believe entrepreneurship can be taught. Both men and women agreed that entrepreneurship is more nurture than nature.

When ranking the reasons to choose entrepreneurship:

- 60 percent of Americans identified self-fulfillment, possibly to realize their own ideas.
- 59 percent said they wanted independence from an employer and to be their own boss.
- 54 percent reported better compatibility of family, leisure time, and career.

The number of people thinking about or already working in their own business is also increasing across demographic groups. According to *The Futurist* magazine, baby boomers, considered to be the healthiest and most educated generation in history, have started retiring from their traditional careers or have been laid off, and a large number have started or will start their own businesses.

Both Gen Xers and millennials are very entrepreneurial in spirit, and they don't hesitate to start their own businesses. Neither Gen Xers nor millennials view starting a business as a risky venture the way many baby boomers might.

Then there are thousands of Americans who have become what the *New York Times* has coined "accidental entrepreneurs." These are people who found themselves out of work with no viable option except to make it on their own through self-employment.

In 2014, there were 28.2 million privately owned businesses in the United States. If you are thinking about starting your own business, what is motivating you to do so? You have heard the cliché "You can be your own boss" touted as the overriding benefit of "running your own show." It is true that you have no one to hold accountable but yourself for what you either achieve or fail to achieve in your own business.

Consider these other reasons:

Catherine, an independent contractor who handles marketing for a catalog company, says, "I like the freedom that comes from working for myself."

Leonard, an author, journalist, and psychotherapist who earned his master's degree in counseling at age fifty-two, says, "I am on my own and am quite aware of the drawbacks, such as a lack of resources and a lonely feeling at times. But I get more of a sense of meaning from my work by being on my own."

Barri worked as chief operating officer of a $12 million start-up company and became ill. She left, took a four-year sabbatical, and then tried to go back to work at a Fortune 500 company. "I knew it was a mistake almost the day I started." Now, says Barri, "I'm back on my own doing business consulting and enjoying it."

Maria runs her own training and consulting business. "Having my own practice allows me the freedom to 'mix and match' my skills and experience. I also have the privilege of organizing my own time and tasks. I work with Japanese companies and often answer e-mails well into the night—but then I have the time in the morning to go to water aerobics and privately teach English as a second language [ESL] students!"

In an article in *Success* magazine, Lori Rosenkopf, assistant professor of management at the Wharton School, says, "You don't have to have misplaced priorities, a dysfunctional personality, and a fanatical work ethic to be a thriving entrepreneur. The creation of value through innovative products and services—the essence of entrepreneurship—can happen for any sort of person. You can be a successful entrepreneur no matter who you are."

Being self-employed can take many different forms, from buying a company or franchise to working as a freelancer or starting a consulting business. Regardless of which of these self-employment options you choose, it is crucial to your success to become very familiar with your preferences, skills, interests, and the areas that you need to develop.

Step 1: Complete the "Yearning to Be on Your Own" Self-Assessment

It is important for you to be clear about your reasons for wanting to be on your own. By revisiting your self-assessment results, you can confirm your strengths, weaknesses, needs, and desires in relation to being on your own.

Review the values you wrote down on page 33. Which ones do you think you can fulfill by being self-employed? Which of these values might not be as easily fulfilled by being on your own?

CHANGE RESILIENCE

How did you score on the change resilience quiz on pages 41–42? As an entrepreneur you will be dealing constantly with change in your business—with your customers and clients, with competitors in the marketplace, and with the economy.

If your score indicated that you have a high level of discomfort with change, think about some ways that you can become more comfortable with change. One suggestion is to start making small changes in your routine starting today. How can you begin to be more comfortable with change?

INTERESTS

Turning an interest into a business is very common. Review the ten interests you listed in the self-assessment you took on page 51. How can you incorporate one or several of these into your own business?

FAVORITE SKILLS

One reason you may want to be on your own is that you have tired of doing work or undertaking projects that aren't interesting to you anymore. While many entrepreneurs will tell you that as a small business owner you will become the "chief cook and bottle washer," you gain a higher level of satisfaction even by doing tedious tasks, because it is your business. Nevertheless, it is important to understand which of your favorite skills you prefer using so that you can plan your entrepreneurial situation more effectively. Review the top ten favorite skills you listed in the self-assessment on pages 58–59. Which of these do you want to spend the majority of your time being involved with? Write them down here.

_____

_____

_____

Having a strong desire to be in your own business is very important. In addition, studies of successful entrepreneurs reveal common characteristics: motivations, attitudes, personality traits, values, and beliefs. How well suited are you to being an entrepreneur? Take this brief quiz to begin to find out.

HOW DO YOU KNOW SELF-EMPLOYMENT IS FOR YOU?

1. Security isn't a very high need of mine.

Agree   *Disagree*

2. I become easily bored with many things I undertake.

Agree   *Disagree*

3. I am willing to commit my savings to starting my own business.

Agree   *Disagree*

4. I am willing to borrow money from others if need be.

Agree   *Disagree*

5. I am very tired of a daily routine and really would like more variety.

Agree   *Disagree*

6. I am willing to work as long and as hard as it takes to reach my goals.

Agree   *Disagree*

7. The idea of selling doesn't scare me.

Agree   *Disagree*

8. I truly see the value of networking and am willing to do it constantly.

Agree   *Disagree*

9. As a child or younger person I started one or several entrepreneurial ventures.

Agree   *Disagree*

10. I enjoy spending time alone.

Agree   *Disagree*

11. I prefer solo or one-on-one activities to group activities.

Agree   *Disagree*

12. My work history shows a consistent pattern of stretching myself by plunging into new situations and learning new skills.

Agree   *Disagree*

13. Although realistic, I'm an optimistic person.

Agree   *Disagree*

14. My spouse or significant other and family are supportive of me.

Agree   *Disagree*

15. I am a decisive person who is willing to make quick decisions even when I don't have all the information.

Agree   *Disagree*

16. I'm usually pretty good about asking other people for help or mentoring when I'm unsure or lack knowledge about something.

Agree   *Disagree*

17. Others describe me as a focused person.

Agree   *Disagree*

18. I am able to motivate myself consistently and maintain a high level of motivation even when under stress.

Agree   *Disagree*

19. I have the emotional ability to bounce back pretty quickly after setbacks or failure.

Agree   *Disagree*

20. When I face problems or challenges, I feel inspired to solve them.

Agree   *Disagree*

SCORE
Now add up the number of Agrees you circled.

15 to 20:   You have the mind-set of an entrepreneur and should be able to achieve wonderful success in your own venture. Although your entrepreneurial instincts are good, be sure to write a solid business plan.

10 to 14:   If you are very thorough about writing a business plan, securing financing, and getting support from your family and network, you have a very good chance for success in your own business.

9 to 13:   While you need to learn more about being self-employed, with focused passion and some education you can be successful. Perhaps you should find a partner or work as a contract employee for additional support first.

5 to 8:   Your skills and attitudes are not indicative of entrepreneurial success. If you are yearning to be on your own, you should seriously consider taking some classes, finding a mentor who is self-employed, and examining your attitudes before taking the plunge.

1 to 4:   Your score indicates that your talents may not lie in the entrepreneurial arena. Take another look at what you

feel is missing in your work and think of a different approach—besides starting a business—to fulfill your needs.

Regardless of whether your score is 20 or 1, if you undertake a business on your own, you will experience many challenges and obstacles along with the joy and rewards. Making a career shift to entrepreneurism is riskier than staying in the corporate world, so be sure to question your own motives carefully.

While many people think that having their own business automatically enables them to earn more money than they ever have before, this may not turn out to be true. While the need to feed and clothe yourself and your family may be very real, a truly successful entrepreneur always has a higher purpose than earning money. You may have decided that starting your own business, rather than working as an employee for someone else, is the only way to fulfill your need for meaning. In fact, 90 percent of the people interviewed for this book who yearned to be self-employed ranked the need to find meaning as having more importance than the desire to earn a lot of money. These individuals realized that they could find their version of meaning more easily through their own business than through someone else's.

Step 2: Exploring Roadblocks and Opportunities

So you've made the decision to strike out on your own. What next? The good news is that there are a number of options to pursue under the umbrella of entrepreneurial ventures:

• You can opt to work as a temporary or interim employee, in either a long-term contract with one company or a series of short stints for many different organizations. Most commonly called freelancing, this is one of the fastest-growing forms of self-employment. You can "hang out your shingle" as a sole practitioner and sell a product or provide a service. The individual who is a sole proprietor is more involved with doing the actual work than in building, growing, and eventually selling a business. Consultants also belong to this group. George Gendron, former editor in chief of *Inc.* magazine, calls this type of individual "a knowledge worker."

• You may decide to join the thousands of entrepreneurs who have purchased franchises. While the concept of a franchise can be appealing because of the brand that is already in place for you and the promise of training and support, there are other factors to consider, such as the up-front investment of capital, the lack of complete control over how you run your business, stiff competition, and the lifestyle of a franchise owner. These are areas you will need to research and think about carefully.

• Buying an established business that is healthy or one that needs turning around is yet another route to take. There are plenty of businesses for sale. Buying a business is sometimes referred to as "secondhand" entrepreneurship because the start-up phase is eliminated.

• Think you have the next great idea? Finding one or more partners and creating a limited partnership or incorporating your business is another choice. If either of these options appeals to you, you are probably serious about building a company. *Shark Tank*, the popular TV reality competition, showcases aspiring entrepreneurs who make presentations to a panel of high-profile, wealthy investors because they are seeking investments for their products and services.

How do you decide which option is right for you? Here are some pros and cons of each of the five types of entrepreneurial ventures described, some assessments to help you determine which route is best for you, as well as some steps you will need to take toward achieving each venture.

Working as a Contractor or Freelancer

As a contractor or freelancer, your focus is on identifying a company that needs your specific set of skills, which enables you to negotiate your compensation as well as how and when you will deliver the work. Your mutual goal is to produce immediate results for the company. The pluses? If you want a flexible schedule, need to beef up your résumé, or are interested in trying out a certain type of work before pursuing it as a full-time employee, then becoming a contractor or freelancer could be the right career move for you.

Ann is a human resources professional. At sixty-two, she has found it increasingly difficult to find full-time employment. Instead, Ann has held a series of contract recruiting positions with various Fortune 500 companies and is thrilled that she can include these blue-chip companies on her résumé. Ann possesses a very marketable skill, and as a result she has had very little "bench time."

Yet, as Ann learned, this type of work has its downside. As a contract worker you don't usually have benefits such as health insurance and paid vacation time, nor do you have the affiliation and status you have as a full-time employee. Any company that hires you as a contractor will expect you to possess state-of-the-art skills in your field, skills that you must acquire on your own time from training that you pay for out of your own pocket. Once your current assignment has ended, you face the challenge of marketing yourself to new prospective employers. Since Ann has had health insurance benefits with only one of the companies she has worked for as a contract recruiter, she worries about having to pay for health coverage at her age. And she is particularly vulnerable to the swings in the economy. During the last recession, when employee layoffs at large corporations occurred, Ann found it more and more difficult to find contract recruiting positions because hiring was limited.

Wally is an accountant who, feeling Bored and Plateaued, finally decided to leave his employer of several years when the company was taken over by new management. Wally made sure that his separation arrangement with his employer included a severance package. Because he was unsure of what he wanted to do next, Wally decided to temp and immediately found an accounting assignment. No sooner did he start his new assignment than he realized the work bored him. Wally fulfilled his time commitment and then began another six-month assignment for a start-up company. This time he is enjoying himself and feels challenged for the first time in years. In fact, Wally is having so much fun that he hasn't decided whether he'll continue working as an independent contractor. Even if he decides to go to work for a company full-time after this assignment ends, Wally will approach the job market with a renewed sense of enthusiasm for his work.

Working as a Sole Practitioner

If you decide to start a business on your own without the structure of a franchise or the support of a partner, you have the advantage of being able to change gears whenever necessary to meet marketplace needs. On the other hand, you'll need to present the professional image of a company despite the fact that you *are* the company.

When you become a sole practitioner, your greatest challenge initially is to decide on, and commit to, what it is you will provide to customers or clients, whether it be a product, a service, or both. While it may be very clear to you that, for example, as a CPA you will provide accounting services, you still need to ask yourself a number of questions. Do you want to specialize in serving individuals or small businesses? If you want to focus on small businesses, do you want to help small businesses in service industries only? What kinds of service industries? Where will you concentrate geographically? Is there a specific type of accounting work that you won't do because you dislike it? Conversely, do you love working in a specific niche of accounting and think you would like to specialize in it?

Answering the following questions carefully will help you narrow your business focus.

1. Do you have specific technical skills and motivated abilities that you would enjoy using in your own business? What are they? Who needs these?

    _____

    _____

_____

_____

2. Is there a glaring need in the marketplace that is either unfilled or burgeoning? If so, what is it?

_____

_____

_____

3. Does a current trend exist in the marketplace that has created a need for, or different approach to, an established product or service? What about an anticipated trend? If so, what is it?

_____

_____

_____

4. Is there a very specific niche that you can fill either because of your unique skills or a market need? What is it?

_____

_____

_____

_____

5. Is there an existing product or service that you know could be improved? Describe it.

_____

_____

_____

6. Is there an established service or product that can be introduced in a different market? What is it?

_____

_____

_____

7. Have you observed recurring buying patterns of individuals or corporations that can create a business opportunity for you? What are they?

_____

_____

_____

8. Is there a business in another country that you could expand globally?

_____

_____

_____

_____

Answering these questions requires some serious thought and market research. It is impossible to really know what the marketplace needs without some investigation to verify your instincts about the needs that exist in your specific area of interest.

Conducting market research is a fancy way to describe the process of finding out what individuals and companies need and are willing to pay for. As a beginning entrepreneur you need to find out very quickly if you have developed a viable business idea, because even if you are in love with your idea, if very few people need it or are willing to pay for it, you will not succeed. This does not mean that you should spend an exorbitant amount of money polling thousands of people. Instead, here are some easy-to-implement ideas for discovering what the market needs and wants:

• Once you have focused on who your target clients might be, ask potential clients the same questions (to create uniformity) one-on-one, in person, or by phone; send surveys via e-mail or using social media. Offer respondents some kind of simple and inexpensive incentive, such as a dollar bill or a book. Encourage anonymity and candid reactions.

• Run several small brainstorming sessions, facilitated by someone other than you, to generate new business ideas.

• Attend trade shows and professional association meetings where clients and other vendors or business owners meet.

• Read trade publications, blogs, and Web sites for market data and trends.

The type of business you operate and the clients you serve now very likely won't be the same in a year or two. Your business will evolve over time to meet marketplace trends and your own preferences and personal needs. Joy's business is a good example. When she started her own business in her early thirties, she was recruiting entry-level salespeople for copier and telecommunication companies, and doing some sales training. Her recruiting activity guaranteed her income because she was able to bring to her own business some of her clients from the contingency agency firm she had worked for as an employee for many years. Over time, Joy began to slow down the recruiting aspect of her business and eventually stopped recruiting altogether. She made a transition into sales training for the publishing industry. More recently she has made the decision to shift away gradually from training toward giving keynote speeches.

As a sole practitioner it isn't necessary to look like a large company by calling yourself president or renting an office at a posh address. What is important is presenting a professional and credible image to your clients. Here's how:

• Use a uniform approach with your marketing materials, including your business cards, social media networking profiles, bio, and Web site.

• Don't print an expensive brochure or other collateral materials, because the services or products you provide can and will change quickly—and so will the clients you work with.

• Use a professional graphic artist to design your logo. A logo is especially important if you use your name as your company name.

• Prepare a statement that succinctly describes your business to clients and anyone who asks what you do. Your statement should briefly explain what you do and effectively describe the benefits you provide to clients: "I offer consulting services to small- and medium-size businesses to help them analyze their utility costs. I then recommend ways to reduce these costs. I guarantee a minimum cost reduction of 10 percent for any client I work with, regardless of their situation or type of business."

• Learn every aspect of running your solo practice well before hiring someone else to do it. This includes bookkeeping, Web site management, proposal writing, and marketing. When you are confident that you can handle these areas, outsource whatever you can afford so that you can focus on developing business and delivering your service or product.

• Read Alan Weiss's book *Million Dollar Consulting*. It is an excellent guide for setting fees and analyzing the profitability of your services.

• Find three to five sole practitioners to share ideas and commiserate with about your businesses.

As a sole practitioner you will continually experiment with how you handle different aspects of your business. Your goal should be to figure out which services or products reap the most satisfaction and profitability for you. Your limitation as a one-person business is that you have a finite amount of time to work, so be smart about managing your time by continually assessing how you spend it.

Purchasing a Franchise

A *franchise* can be described as an ongoing relationship between a *franchisor* (the granter of the franchise) and a *franchisee* (the person who is granted the franchise), which involves rights to products and services, a trademark identity, and business concepts, including a marketing and distribution system. In other words, as a franchisee you are investing your assets in a brand and a system.

What's the upside? A franchise can provide you with quicker start-up success, a faster way to access capital to expand your business, increased earnings, and marketing strength.

The cons? You have to invest a significant amount of capital up front, and your control of what you consider *your* business is restricted by the franchisor. Innovation isn't always possible within the structure of the franchisor's system. You also may discover that the business doesn't truly match your lifestyle or skills.

Bill Anderson was forty-four when he bought three Mail Boxes Etc. (MBE) stores in Philadelphia and southern New Jersey. Of the thirty-five hundred MBE franchises in the United States, his stores ranked in the top fifty in sales. When Bill started exploring the possibility of owning his own business, he didn't plan to be a franchisee. Instead, he saw a need for a place where the average consumer could go to make copies, send packages, and pick up mail, as an alternative to the post office. He himself had used MBE and loved the concept. When he decided to start this type of business after researching his entrepreneurial options, Bill concluded that owning a franchise offered the most promising opportunity.

Bill's advice to anyone thinking about buying a franchise is to "buy a business, not a job." In other words, as he puts it, if you are looking for a place to go every day where your definition of marketing is locking and unlocking the door, you'll never be successful as a franchisee.

Bill is adamant about the importance of believing in the specific product or service that a franchise offers customers rather than simply buying a franchise because you can afford it. Buying a quick oil change franchise when you know nothing about cars and hate to get your hands dirty is not a recipe for success. Neither is buying a sandwich franchise when you don't enjoy dealing with food or the public.

When Bill decided that MBE was the way to go, he immediately began to develop a relationship with the local MBE store owner in his hometown. Bill took him to lunch and gradually, as the owner began to trust Bill, he shared important financial information with him. The owner showed Bill his monthly royalty report, and Bill analyzed the financials, including the revenue stream, the average fixed and variable expenses, and the payroll costs.

Once Bill felt comfortable that he could satisfy his income needs as an MBE franchise owner, he purchased the closest available store to his home. He became actively involved in the International Franchise Organization as a board member and even appeared in a Super Bowl commercial in 1999 as part of MBE's "See Your Small Business on the Super Bowl Search" campaign.

Now sixty-six and wanting to redirect his efforts, in 2014, Bill sold his two Philadelphia stores (now UPS stores), and his New Jersey store is currently up for sale. He says that his experience owning franchises was easily the most interesting time in his career.

Bill Brimmer (another Bill) is a senior franchise adviser for FranNet (a franchise brokerage) who counsels people who are considering buying a franchise. He shares some interesting facts about franchising:

Franchising provides more than twenty-one million jobs, with more than 900,000 operating units in 3,100 franchise companies across more than eighty industries. Franchising is a $2.3 trillion business with nearly $700 billion in annual payrolls.

Food franchises are the most popular type of franchise; however, both the investment and rate of failure are the highest for this type. In general, service businesses are more successful. These can include hair care, spas, commercial and residential cleaning, signage (still the most popular form of advertising), expense reduction, security, pet grooming, senior care, window-treatment sales and installation, insect prevention, dry cleaning, tutoring, and sales training.

If you are seriously considering becoming a franchisee, you should be able to answer the following ten questions affirmatively:

1. Do you have the kind of personality that can accept running your business according to someone else's plan without feeling that it will compromise your individuality?
2. Does each of the franchises you are looking at have a readily identifiable brand name and goodwill associated with it?
3. Will the franchise you are considering be an enjoyable place to own, manage, and work day to day, possibly for years?
4. Are you prepared to spend the time doing research by calling as many franchises as you can (at least ten) and visiting as many operating units as possible?
5. Would you feel proud of the product or service you are selling?
6. Is the product or service recession-proof?
7. Is the franchisor strategically minded, rather than just focused on market presence? Can he or she clearly communicate this strategy to you?
8. Have you researched the competition in your area, and do you feel comfortable with the potential market?
9. Do you understand the extent of operations assistance that is available?

10. Have you found a reputable lawyer who has experience with franchise agreements?

Buying a Business

BizBuySell is a popular resource for potential business purchasers and business owners who are selling their businesses. The opportunities for you to buy a business are varied. The challenge is, of course, to find the right one for you.

Glen Cooper is a nationally known business broker, business coach, and motivational speaker. He explains the key reasons to buy an existing business:

1. You will inherit an established client base.
2. You may be able to retain experienced and loyal employees.
3. More favorable financing terms are available to you as the buyer of an established business, which can include seller financing, bank financing, and even financing by vendors.
4. An existing business has an accepted product or service, which defines its market position.
5. Established sales and marketing, accounting, inventory tracking, and payroll and production systems are all in place.

If you have done your homework on the company you are thinking of buying and all these things are truly in place, you will certainly jump-start your chances for success.

There are, however, some downsides to buying an existing business:

• The process of researching a business is tedious and taxing, especially if you aren't highly analytical or adept at interpreting financial data.
• Finding the right business that will complement your professional experience, skills, and resources can be challenging. If you have spent your entire career in a service industry, for example, it may not make sense to consider buying a manufacturing company because of the steep learning curve involved.

• Even with the assistance of experts such as lawyers, accountants, insurance agents, and bankers (all of which you should take advantage of), it isn't always easy to uncover any serious problems in the company you are considering buying. Here are some examples of common problems that are difficult to expose: inflated income, substantial debt, and assets that have been pledged as collateral.

• A seller often inflates the value of equipment. Always hire an independent appraiser to assess its value. If the seller of a business tells you that another buyer is about to make an offer, don't let this rush you or distract you from making a careful decision.

• Accounts-receivable problems are a common issue for most small businesses at various times. Reviewing invoices going back at least six months to identify late payers will help you become aware of cash-flow history and any credit problems.

Here are some questions that can help you decide whether buying a business is the right choice for you and what you should consider in the search process.

1. What has your professional experience included (retail, manufacturing, service, finance, high tech, etc.)?

_____

_____

_____

2. How long do you want to spend searching for the right business to buy? How many hours a day or week are you willing to commit?

_____

_____

_____

_____

3. Are you willing to move or commute a long distance if necessary?

_____

_____

_____

4. How involved with the management of your business do you want to be? Do you see your role as an investor only, as the person who hires the people who will run it day to day, or as the one who will step in as the hands-on leader?

_____

_____

_____

_____

5. Do you have a strong network of advisers, vendors or suppliers, and potential clients in certain industries? Who are they?

_____

_____

_____

_____

6. How large do you want your business to be?

_____

_____

_____

_____

7. Do you want a business that has had steady growth with a stable cash flow or one that has more growth potential and not as consistent a cash flow?

_____

_____

_____

8. Are you interested in buying a company that needs to be turned around?

_____

_____

_____

_____

9. How much cash do you have available, including potential assets, profit sharing, stocks and bonds, and savings that you can liquidate to invest in a business?

_____

_____

_____

_____

10. Do you have contacts with bankers, venture capitalists, or private-equity investors? Who are they?

_____

_____

_____

11. How soon do you need to see profits?

_____

_____

_____

While these are some guidelines to contemplate, be careful not to narrow your search too much. There are many complementary industries that you may not have thought about. For example, if you're a sports enthusiast, instead of looking only at sporting goods stores, why not consider buying a small magazine or Web site that specializes in sports?

If you don't know where you can find businesses that are for sale, here are some suggestions:

- Talk to your professional network, friends, and acquaintances.
- Seek out trusted advisers such as your attorney, accountant, banker, doctor, or dentist.

- Trade associations can be very helpful if you have narrowed down your search to the type of industry you're interested in. They all have local meetings, and many have online newsletters or Web sites.
- Cold-calling owners of businesses can sometimes uncover businesses for sale that haven't yet been advertised or listed with a broker. You can find the names of companies on local chamber of commerce membership lists or simply by driving through commercial areas and writing down names.
- Read newspaper and trade publication advertisements.
- Search the Internet by industry or business broker. Or look at the Web sites of businesses in which you are interested.
- Use a business broker, but understand that brokers nearly always represent the seller of a business, not the buyer. A successful business broker will offer you a large selection of listings or specialize in the area you've targeted.

Remember: If the owner of a company has never sold a business before, he or she can tend to overvalue the business *and* be emotional in the process. Doing your homework thoroughly costs money and takes time but is well worth it in the long run. If you are organized in your approach, however, you may become the proud owner of an established and profitable business. Remember the number of small businesses cited at the beginning of this chapter? More than twenty-eight million businesses—and all you need is one!

Creating a Partnership

Finding the right person to partner with in your own business is analogous to getting married. To be successful you want to have the same values, be compatible day to day, and accept each other's limitations while leveraging strengths. Most important, you must trust each other.

You may already have a business idea and have decided to find a partner, or you may be talking to someone about first becoming business partners and then identifying the type of business you'd like to start. Either way, you should be extremely cautious about the person you will probably spend more time with than your spouse. Some suggestions for assessing your prospective business partner are these:

- Collaborate with him or her on a project or a cross-selling effort before committing to a full-time partnership. Doing this will give you the chance to observe the other person's working style and see how he or she handles business overall.
- Have a serious discussion about each other's vision for your business. Are they in sync or worlds apart?
- Be careful about partnering with someone who is too similar to you. Be sure your prospective business partner has strengths and expertise that you don't possess, and vice versa.
- Be very sure that your partner will take the financial and legal responsibilities of starting a business seriously.
- Have a discussion about who will be in charge of each area of the company.
- Once you've decided to proceed with your partnership, write down your expectations of each other about responsibilities and tasks.
- Hire a lawyer to draft a partnership agreement for you and include in it the most important component: a mechanism for ending your partnership.
- Investigate the legal and tax implications of a general partnership, a corporation, and a limited liability corporation before deciding on the one to use for your business.

A business partnership requires constant communication and hard work; however, it can be very rewarding to have a partner who shares your dream of running a successful business.

Roadblocks and Obstacles

All potential entrepreneurs can encounter roadblocks or obstacles regardless of which route they take. You can address them, however, so that you can deal with them ahead of time.

Selling. Whether you like it or not, when you are an entrepreneur, *you are always selling.* Your perseverance at sales and your ability to sell will be one of the most critical factors in your success. "Attitudes and Behaviors That Create Small Business Success," a survey conducted by Yankelovich, a market research company, found that a dominant concern of the more than two thousand entrepreneurs questioned was attracting and keeping clients, outranking worries about staffing, paying the bills, and competition.

Unfortunately, unless you have worked in sales or have been responsible for revenue as a sales manager, the whole area of sales may be foreign to you. Whether you lack experience, have a dislike for the act of selling, or don't think it is how you should be spending your time, it is important that you overcome your specific emotional and practical obstacles and embrace the idea that as an entrepreneur you are a professional salesperson.

If necessary, you can hire a sales coach who specializes in working with small business owners, or you can take classes or workshops offered by private companies and colleges and universities. Hundreds of books have been written on the subject, many of which are geared toward the person who has never sold anything before.

If you are sure that you want to go into your own business, you should begin your education in sales. Waiting until the day you open your doors doesn't make good sense. The best way to become a good salesperson is to sell and keep selling. Start now by selling your business idea to others.

If you have both a marketing plan and sales goals (the basic components of a business plan; see "Marketing Plan" on pages 176–177) and feel passionate about your business, selling will not be as difficult as you think. Sales techniques are learned like any other technical ability, and success is a matter of using specific skills rather than a reflection of how dynamic, extroverted, and bright you are. One of the greatest challenges an entrepreneur faces is maintaining sales activity while fulfilling orders or delivering service. If you have ever taken a Sales 101 course, you know that the pipeline of prospective clients must constantly be fed. Doing this successfully requires focus and discipline above all else.

Cash flow. One of the biggest worries that most people have about starting their own business is giving up a steady salary. There is also anxiety about not being able to pay their bills, both personally and professionally. This is a valid concern. In a perfect world, having twelve to eighteen months' worth of cash put away in anticipation of the ups and downs of a new business (or any business for that matter) should solve the problem. But the truth is that most people don't have the ability to save that much money and end up starting their business with a smaller financial cushion. So what's the answer? If delaying the start-up of your business for six or eight months means you'll be able to save more money, then this is a wise strategy. If your fear about not having enough money is paralyzing you from moving forward, however, then set a goal for starting your business within a specific time frame and don't let yourself off the hook.

Most people who start a business do so with savings, credit card cash advances, loans from friends and family, and severance payments. The reality is that you will be able to invest only what you have at your disposal, and this must be an amount that is comfortable for you.

Elizabeth started her business with money from a 401(k) plan from her last employer. This provided her with a sum to pay all her expenses for four months. Most financial planners or accountants would not recommend this strategy, but it was Elizabeth's only viable option at the time. Did it create stress for her knowing that she was operating in a four-month window? Absolutely! Yet Elizabeth also knew that she could borrow money from several friends if the need arose. Her fear motivated her to hustle and drum up business quickly, which she did. She had gone through the process of budgeting every single expense and was more aware of how much it cost for her to live and work than ever before in her life.

The following are some procedures you can put in place to help your cash-flow stream once you're in business:

- Offer a small discount for early or on-time payment. Most accounts payable departments are trained to treat early-payment invoices as a priority.
- Request a deposit for project work or a large contract. Be sure to have your client sign a contract stating the exact terms of their payment for your products or services.
- Ask for a monthly retainer for ongoing work. This also delivers the message to your client that you value your relationship and assures your availability.
- Arrange follow-up services or products as part of the overall package you sell to your client. Obviously, in addition to helping your cash flow, you are creating residual revenue.
- Be sure you are charging fair market fees and prices. Just because you are new in your business does not mean that you should undercut your prices. Ask your competition about their pricing and ask your clients what they pay your competition.
- Have a set of goals and a strategy in place for collecting cash, including a plan for seriously delinquent payments. Don't be afraid to use outside assistance if you need to.

Lack of a support system, resources, and feedback. As an entrepreneur, it can be very lonely not to have people and resources surrounding you when you need them the most. Even if you are running a company with employees, they won't necessarily be able to provide you with the support you'll need. This means that you should immediately find or create external opportunities to supply you with this often unfulfilled need.

Networking is necessary to your success as an entrepreneur for generating sales leads. It is also a wonderful vehicle for finding other people who are in situations like your own to compare notes with and learn from. There are many structured networking groups and associations both local and national in scope. Find out what they are by asking everyone you know which groups they belong to and which ones they find most valuable. Don't just network when business is slow or when you're feeling guilty about not doing it. Make it part of your weekly schedule.

Creating a small advisory board of people who are at various levels of experience in running their own businesses is a fabulous way to learn and share your experiences. You can schedule formal meetings or communicate more informally on an as-needed basis.

Hiring a business coach who specializes in working with start-up business owners or established business owners will provide ongoing support that you will take seriously because you are paying for it.

Involve your family in your business. You will work much harder than you ever did before, and whether you like it or not, this will eat into your family and personal time. Asking your family for advice or a different perspective helps them feel included in your business, and often they will surprise you with some great ideas.

Blending your work and your life. There is no question that if you want to be successful in your own business, you will work harder and longer than you ever did as an employee. The time you spend with work and leisure will blur, partially because of technology that enables you to work twenty-four hours a day, but also because you can always be doing something else to take care of your business. Even if you have an attorney, an accountant, a payroll service, an assistant, and a bookkeeper, you are now wearing every single functional hat in your company. If you are not planning, you are selling; if you are not updating your Web site, you are solving a problem— and on and on.

Before you start your business, write down how much time (in hours) you spend a week or month involved with the following categories. If you are not sure, then track a typical week to find out. Next to that number write down how much time you would like to spend doing those things when you start your own business.

Work _____

Commuting to work _____

Outside interests/hobbies/sports _____

Exercise _____

Vacation _____

Family and relatives _____

Religious and spiritual activities _____

Volunteer work _____

Personal business_____

Other (add your own) _____

Refer to this list every three months to see if you have been able to maintain the balance you would like to have in your life as a new entrepreneur. Getting a new business up and running is, at least initially, a twenty-four-hour proposition, and finding "true" balance may not be possible for a while.

Step 3: Create an Action Plan

A Vision Statement for Your Business

It is extremely important to remember that success is, as the cliché goes, "in the eye of the beholder." Most likely your vision of success varies greatly from your neighbor's vision. What is important is that before you start your own business, you are able to articulate your vision—to yourself and to your family. In just a moment you'll learn how to write a business plan in which you'll include many of your specific measurable goals. While your revenue and income and the number of clients you serve are certainly important, they are only a part of how you'll define and measure your success. Developing a brief written vision statement for your business is a good way to capture your business concept. This vision is what you would like your business to become; it often includes your unique selling proposition, more commonly known as USP. Your USP is that characteristic or feature that differentiates your business from your competition.

An example of a vision statement: To be recognized nationally as a leader in presentation skills services by providing innovative training, coaching, facilitating, and consulting services to our clients.

What is your vision statement?

_____

_____

_____

_____

Writing a Business Plan

Unless freelancing is your self-employment choice, writing a business plan is very important for any other type of business you are starting. This is a required document if you are seeking external financial assistance, whether you are approaching a bank, private investor, or a venture capitalist. Even if you are relying solely on your personal assets to finance your business, the process that you go through to write your plan is as valuable as the outcome itself. A business plan is a road map for your success as an entrepreneur. Software is available for you to use as a template for your business plan, and there are innumerable books you can read on the subject. These are the basic components of every plan: a company overview, executive summary, marketing plan, management plan, and financial plan.

COMPANY OVERVIEW—The company overview includes both short- and long-term projections of sales, profits, market penetration, and any other measures of progress of the success of your business. The type of business you are becoming involved with (buying a business, buying a franchise, or starting a business from scratch) and the way you plan to structure the company are also part of the company overview. With the advice of a lawyer and an accountant, you may want to become a limited liability corporation (LLC or sole proprietorship), a partnership, or an "S" or "C" corporation. The way you structure your company is important for liability and tax issues. Pages 276–278 in the resources guide lists books that will give you guidance in this area.

Additionally, you should list the type of taxes you'll pay as a business and as an employer, as well as all legal requirements such as licensing and local, state, and federal regulations and laws. The last two items to be included in the overview are the kinds and amount of insurance protection you'll need along with the types of advisers with whom you plan to consult.

EXECUTIVE SUMMARY—This is a brief (no more than three pages) opening description written to grab the reader's attention. It is a snapshot of your company, including the market opportunity you are pursuing, your product or service, facts and figures about your target clients, a competitive strategy, your management team (if relevant), and a financial summary. Since this is the most difficult and the most important part of your business plan to write, you should write it last.

MARKETING PLAN—The best way to describe the marketing plan is that it indicates how you'll take in money. While the word "marketing" is used, this portion of your business plan is primarily focused on selling. It outlines how you propose to sell your products or services, how you plan to bring them to the attention of prospective clients, and at what price. To write your marketing plan, ask yourself the following questions:

> What product do you plan to make or sell, or what service do you plan to provide?

> To whom (prospective clients) do you hope to sell your product, and why will they buy it?

> How many prospective clients are there, and where are they?

> What is your competition, and how will you capture a share of the market?

> What prices or fees do you plan to charge, and how did you calculate them?

> How and where will you deliver your products or services?

> How will you promote your new business (social media, advertising, direct selling, networking, etc.)?

> How will you keep your clients happy (deal with complaints, provide customer service)?

MANAGEMENT PLAN—While your marketing plan describes how you'll take in money, the management plan describes how you are going to spend it as well as how you will structure and operate your business. Write your management plan using the following questions as guidelines:

> What will you name your business? GoDaddy is the number one site for searching for and purchasing Internet domain names and Web site hosting. You can choose to register your name with the US Patent and Trademark Office, which will

keep your company name protected anywhere in the United States and on the Internet.

How will you manage your business day to day?

Where will you locate your business? This may be crucial for a restaurant, for example, but not important for a sole proprietor or consultant.

What equipment and furniture will you need, and how much will they cost?

What kind of phone service and office equipment will you need, and how much will they cost?

Will you need materials or inventory, and who will supply them and at what price?

Do you plan to hire employees? What skills and qualifications will they need? How much will you pay them?

What records will you keep? How will you keep track of taxes, insurance, lease information, employee payroll and benefits, and so on?

Who will do your bookkeeping and accounting?

FINANCIAL PLAN—This translates your business into dollars and cents. It spells out how much you think it will cost to get started and operate for one or more years, how much you think you'll need to take in from sales, and how much you will need to borrow to make your entrepreneurial vision a reality.

You should detail your costs of operating for the first year or until the break-even point. This should include every item that will cost your business money: rent, utilities, taxes, salaries, employee benefits, postage, marketing costs, office supplies, and so forth. Include everything! You will develop this information by preparing a budget for your start-up year and each year thereafter.

You should present how much money you expect to take in during your first year in business or until you break even, and the total amount you will need to get started and keep your business functioning.

The amount of money you plan to invest from your own resources—savings, credit card cash advances, a severance payment, or refinancing your mortgage (home-equity loan)—and the amount you will borrow from friends and family should be listed.

If you are planning to borrow money from your bank or another outside source, it will be interested in all the information in your business plan and what your business experience and management capabilities are. It will also ask for a financial statement covering your personal assets, liabilities, and any collateral you are prepared to invest.

You can attach supporting documents such as résumés and bios; references from creditors, potential clients, and suppliers; a lease agreement; relevant contracts; partnership agreements; and documentation of your company structure.

Even if you choose not to write a business plan when you are starting your business, it will prove to be a tremendously helpful exercise when you're thinking of expanding your business or are experiencing problems in your business or if you decide to take a more strategic approach to running your business. Obviously, it is optimum to write a business plan when starting from the ground up, but not everyone does so.

Twenty-six Things You Should Do
When Starting Your Business

As you start planning your new business, here are some of the things you should do. Please note that these suggestions are not in any order, nor are they relevant to every type of entrepreneurial venture. Check off each one as you do it.

☐ 1. Interview three entrepreneurs and ask them to share their best advice with you.

☐ 2. Identify your business niche and write a brief mission statement explaining your niche. Also known as your "two-minute drill" or your defining statement, this is different from your company vision.

☐ 3. Obtain two or three referrals to accountants and bookkeepers. Meet and interview them.

☐ 4. Do the same for an attorney and for a certified financial planner (CFP).

☐ 5. Get a long-term disability policy before you quit your job.

☐ 6. Investigate your health insurance options.

☐ 7. Name your business. Register your business name in your county or state or federally, depending upon where you plan on doing business; find and register your business name as a domain name on GoDaddy.com or a similar hosting site.

☐ 8. Decide on your business structure now. Will your business be an LLC, a partnership, or a "C" or an "S" corporation? Go to Nolo.com for more information.

☐ 9. Get an employer identification number (EIN) for IRS purposes. Visit irs.gov or ask your accountant how to do this.

☐ 10. Get licenses and permits. Depending on your business, you can contact your city's business license department, the city zoning board, or the health department.

☐ 11. Build a Web site. WordPress.com is very user-friendly, or you may hire a Web designer.

☐ 12. List your personal assets.

☐ 13. Make a budget for your personal expenses.

☐ 14. If you need financing, get it while you are still working.

☐ 15. Find a location. If you are planning to work from home, check IRS requirements. If you need retail or commercial space, consider accessibility, proximity to competitors, taxes, insurance, utilities, and maintenance.

☐ 16. Open a business checking account.

☐ 17. Research equipment. You may need a computer, printer, scanner, DSL or cable line, copier, phone, postage meter, and smartphone, among other things.

☐ 18. Be sure you have technical support lined up for all your equipment.

☐ 19. Find a graphic artist to design your logo, business cards, and stationery, and get them printed.

☐ 20. Find suppliers through trade shows, buyers' directories, trade publications, the Internet, and referrals.

☐ 21. Open a merchant account so you can accept credit cards. There are dozens of credit card processors to choose from, so be sure to research payment security and compliance standards, Web and mobile payment solutions, costs, and customer service quality.

☐ 22. Create a credit application for customers.

☐ 23. Advertise job openings on Craigslist, LinkedIn, or job boards.

☐ 24. Create a job application, making sure it meets legal guidelines.

☐ 25. Get relevant business insurance, such as workers' compensation, professional liability/errors and omissions, property/casualty, and auto.

☐ 26. Start networking and generating business. Track your activity using sales software or an Excel spreadsheet at a minimum.

The beauty of starting your own business is that it's yours to do with what you want. As an entrepreneur you'll have your unique fingerprint on your business. Here are two success stories to illustrate the point.

When Sergei graduated from the University of Pennsylvania Law School, his family was so proud of him. As Russian emigrants, they moved to the United States when Sergei was very young. Education is an important value for them and knowing that Sergei would become a lawyer fulfilled their dreams for him. Sergei worked as an associate for three big law firms; however, he never felt satisfied. He was spending all his time writing briefs that meant nothing to him, he didn't ever talk to clients, and he had no idea how the work he did fit into the big picture.

During this time, Sergei went on vacation with a friend and his friend's mother, who is a dentist. Sergei asked her if she liked being a dentist. "Very much," she replied. "I deal with patients, manage my practice, handle marketing, and, best of all, I don't have a boss, and I have great flexibility." "What about drilling into people's teeth?" Sergei asked. Her response: "I don't spend that much time doing that." Sergei suddenly realized that it wasn't practicing law that he disliked, but the way he was doing it. He immediately started a solo practice specializing in lemon law. Nine years later, at forty-one years old, Sergei has an international law firm specializing in consumer rights with twenty full-time and five part-time employees as well as numerous subcontractors. He is happy and successful, and he spends his time traveling, managing his law practice, marketing, and working on big class-action cases.

After eleven years with Citibank, Sheri resigned from her position as a vice president and started a business, Cotton Candy Kids, which designs and creates custom children's accessories. Sheri expresses well what so many entrepreneurs feel: "Cotton Candy Kids is a perfect blend for me at this time in my life. It allows me to stay home with my children, put my creative 'juices' to work, have a sense of accomplishment, meet new people, and keep the brain working! I have always loved sewing and needed a creative outlet. Someone once told me, 'When you do what you love for a living, it's as easy as breathing.' The business has really taken off, and the path has felt as natural as breathing. It rejuvenates my mind and soul."

The process of starting a business can be overwhelming, and you will find very quickly that some entrepreneurial options are a better fit for you than others. Once you have identified the one or two options you'd like to explore, do the first thing on the list of twenty-six suggestions you just read: Find several people who are doing what you think you'd like to do and talk to them about their experience and recommendations they have for you to get started.

CHAPTER 10

One Toe in the Retirement Pool

Nonprofit group Transamerica Center for Retirement Studies (TCRS) released a report in late 2014 that examined baby boomers' vision for retirement and found that 65 percent plan to work past age sixty-five in their current roles or do not plan to retire at all, and 52 percent plan to continue working in another type of job after they retire from their full-time position. Another survey of strictly middle-income-earning baby boomers conducted by LifeHealthPro.com, also in late 2014, puts the number higher, with nine in ten working baby boomers expecting to work past the conventional retirement age of sixty-five.

In the dictionary, retirement is defined as "going away from business or public life" or "concluding one's working or professional life." Yet all indicators point to a new definition of the word now and in the future. For most baby boomers, retirement is no longer a point in time when someone immediately stops working. It is now a phased transition, which may involve shifting from full-time to part-time work, taking on a position that is more satisfying and less demanding, or pursuing an encore career, according to Catherine Collinson, president of TCRS.

Merrill Lynch and Age Wave surveyed more than seven thousand respondents in 2014 for a report called *Work in Retirement:*

Myths and Motivations to explore and challenge commonly held beliefs about work during retirement. What they found turned the old model of retirement upside down. They identified four phases:

Preretirement: Five years before retiring, 37 percent who want to work in retirement will have already taken some meaningful steps to prepare for their postretirement career, and this number increases to 54 percent among those within two years of retirement.

Career intermission: Most preretirees do not seek to go directly from preretirement to retirement work, because they want a break, a sabbatical, or time to relax and recharge. The timing of this career intermission averages 2.5 years.

Reengagement: This phase lasts nine years on average and includes a blend of work and leisure. In these "flex careers," 83 percent of people tend to work part-time versus 17 percent working full-time, and they are three times more likely to be self-employed.

Leisure: This fourth phase of retirement is focused on rest, relaxation, socializing, traveling, and other priorities that are not related to working. People enter this phase at a point when they are expecting health challenges or simply don't enjoy working anymore.

Today, age is not necessarily an indicator that you should retire. Someone who retires at age sixty-five could have twenty or more years left to live. And according to the US Census Bureau, the sixty-five-and-older segment of the population will increase to seventy-two million in 2030.

If you are eyeing "retirement" in the next several years or are about to retire now and still want to work in some way, the first step is to think long and hard about why you are considering retirement. Among your reasons may be the following:

1. You are simply ready to retire. You have thought about it for a while, and although you aren't necessarily sure about what you'll

do when you retire, you know that it's time. You have tired of the grind of working or have had numerous unhappy job situations and just don't want to participate in the battle that work can be at times.

John, at fifty-six, manages a worldwide business for a health-care company in the areas of clinical diagnostics and marketing and has worked since he was sixteen and a half. He just isn't interested in working anymore. He thinks about retirement constantly and believes that many of his peers are doing so as well.

2. Your spouse or significant other is in the same stage of life as you and is also ready to retire or has done so recently. While it isn't necessary to retire side by side with your partner, the adjustment period that goes along with not working full-time and changing your lifestyle is easier to go through with someone else. Surrounding yourself with friends, former colleagues, relatives, and peers to socialize with and count on as a support group makes retirement so much more pleasurable. If you know enough people who are in the same phase of life that you are, retiring can be even more attractive.

3. You want to retire while you're still in good health so that you can fully enjoy your retirement years. Even if you are in good physical shape now, you may experience health problems as a result of normal aging, some of which you won't be able to anticipate or control. On the other hand, if you are not as healthy as you used to be, retirement is less stressful than working full-time. As the saying goes, "If you don't have your health, you don't have anything."

4. You are reasonably comfortable with the financial aspects of retirement. Income and finances are usually the first thing that people focus on when thinking about taking this step—not surprisingly, since these are also the topics that cause the most concern. Many people do not have a company pension plan, and many others have experienced unforeseen financial reversals in their lives, such as failed investments or shifts in the stock market, or simply haven't saved enough to feel comfortable giving up their current salary. The majority of people retiring will suffer a drop in income no matter what their situation is. While John fantasizes about retiring, he knows that in

order to live the lifestyle he and his wife desire, he can't realistically retire until he's sixty-two. "Having enough to live on with what we have stored away" is his serious concern. He is willing to "hang in there" for another six years in order to ensure that this will happen.

5. Family issues such as caring for your elderly parents and spending quality time with your grandchildren have become more important. While the focus of this chapter is on older individuals, this category also includes those who aren't necessarily older but have found it too difficult to effectively manage both a career and a family. Keri, only thirty-four, loved her career as a vice president of recruiting for an investment bank but has decided to "retire" to spend time with her children and husband. "I found a lot of satisfaction in managing a career and love my time now with my family. I'd like to try to have both but am not sure I can do it and feel satisfied or competent at both."

6. You have a lot of hobbies and interests you yearn to become more involved with, or you'd like to develop certain skills or expertise that you haven't taken the time to do while working.

7. You want to make a career change into another field or industry and simply don't have the time to make this transition while you are working in your current job.

University of Connecticut researchers at the Goldenson Center for Actuarial Research released a new tool in 2015 called the National Retirement Sustainability Index. This tool measures an individual's financial readiness for retirement and is fundamentally different from traditional predictors because it is the first such tool to incorporate noneconomic factors in its calculation. Typically, the standard way to measure an individual's ability to retire simply compares their current net assets with the projected value of those assets in the future. The problem with this is that these projections are hugely dependent upon the performance of financial markets.

This new index adds four factors to the basic model of readiness: your state of health, your job satisfaction, the level of financial planning you have already done, and your level of adaptability. Adaptability refers to your ability and interest in doing other work after retirement.

Several or all of these reasons can significantly influence why, when, and how you choose to "retire." Take some time to think about each one and decide its relevance to your specific situation.

Step 1: Complete the "One Toe in the Retirement Pool" Self-Assessment

Retiring from your current full-time career will enable you to be flexible about the kind of work you'll do and how you'll do it, giving you the opportunity to explore interests, hobbies, or another kind of work.

Review your top ten values on page 33 to remind yourself of what's important to you.

Next, review the interests and favorite skills you wrote down on pages 51 and 58–59, as they will provide the foundation for the type of work you'll find or create. Are there several interests you'd like to get involved with when you retire? Write them down here.

_____

_____

_____

_____

Now do the same for your favorite skills. List the ones that you would like to use for the first time or continue using once you've created your retired life.

_____

_____

_____

_____

Now, keeping your self-assessment results in mind, ask yourself, "If I could do any work in the world after I 'retire,' what would it be? Where would I do it? With whom would I be doing it?"

_____

_____

_____

_____

Once you have refamiliarized yourself with the results of your self-assessment, it's time to do some thinking and exploring about your retirement.

Answering these simple questions can help you ascertain the additional soul-searching and research you need to do to help you plan for retirement:

1. Have you always thought you'd retire at a certain age? If so, what is it?

_____

2. What are or were your reasons for picking this age?

_____

_____

_____

_____

3. Have you already met with a financial adviser to plan for retirement?

_____

4. If not, why haven't you?

_____

_____

_____

_____

5. Do you have an up-to-date will, a revocable trust, and appropriate insurance coverage for you and your family?

_____

_____

_____

6. How do you feel about retiring? Have you really sat down and thought through the possible positive and negative implications of it?

_____

_____

_____

_____

7. Can you picture what retirement would look like for you from a lifestyle standpoint (where you'll live, your proximity to your family, etc.)?

_____

_____

_____

_____

8. Have you had a serious discussion with your spouse and immediate family about retiring?

_____

9. If so, what are their concerns about it?

_____

10. If not, when do you plan to do so?

_____

_____

_____

11. Do you know others who have retired within the last several years? If so, have you had an earnest conversation with them about what they've experienced so far?

_____

_____

12. Have you talked with your employer to explore opportunities for continued work on a more flexible basis, or to engage in work you may find more motivating such as phased retirement, a part-time position, consulting, seasonal work, a sabbatical, or a role as a mentor?

_____

_____

_____

_____

Retirement as we've known it is being transformed into a different type of transition phase. You must prepare yourself emotionally, psychologically, and financially for this new chapter in your life whether it means you're working or not. To do so you must talk to people, research, and be very thoughtful about who you are. You must know what your goals are in life and what makes you happy as well as fulfilled. Nowadays it is quite likely that you will live a very long time after you "retire."

Step 2: Exploring Roadblocks and Opportunities

Your Finances

An April 2014 survey by Gallup revealed that 59 percent of Americans say that they are either very worried or moderately worried about not having enough money for retirement. A Harris Poll conducted for Wells Fargo in late 2014 on the topic of saving for retirement cited that 22 percent of middle-class Americans say that "they would rather die early" than not have enough money to live comfortably in retirement.

Your retirement income will be financed by any investments you may have, Social Security, pension plans, real estate, savings, and income you generate from working. You may not have all these sources of income when you retire, so planning how much you will have is very important.

The majority of workers regard phased retirement plans as important; however, survey results vary widely as to whether employers offer these to employees. Phased retirement plans allow older workers to leave a company gradually over a period of five years or so while their employer distributes the worker's pension withdrawal, compensation, and medical benefits incrementally over time. The 2014 Society for Human Resource Management Employee Benefits report found that overall, 11 percent of organizations offered some type of phased retirement with only 4 percent offering a formal phased retirement program. According to the National Study of Employers, 54 percent of organizations offer all or at least some employees the opportunity to phase into retirement by working reduced hours over a period of time prior to full retirement, while 18 percent allow all or most employees to phase into retirement. Whatever the statistics, it seems clear that many employees lack their employers' support in regards to moving into retirement. And it is uncertain whether employers are considering phased retirement programs in the future.

The sad truth is that many people who retire depend almost solely on Social Security for income, despite the fact that it was never intended to provide 100 percent of a retiree's income. In fact, in 2014, according to the US Social Security Administration, 47 percent of unmarried persons and 22 percent of married couples rely on Social Security for 90 percent or more of their income. On top of this dismal reality, Social Security has been challenged for a long time, and the future looks uncertain unless the entire system is overhauled. According to the Social Security Administration, the current system is not sustainable over the long term at the current benefit and tax rates without large infusions of additional revenue. When the program began in 1935, the ratio of workers funding Social Security was fifty workers to every one retiree. The ratio of workers to retirees in 2025 is projected to be two to one. Not only can these facts about Social Security be ignored, it is advisable that when calculating the retirement income you'll need, you should also factor in a longer-than-usual life span, inflation, and the fact that your money will keep working for you while you are retired.

One way to ease your financial worries for retirement is to hire a financial adviser. When you are selecting a financial adviser, use the following criteria:

1. Was he or she referred to you by someone you know and trust?
2. Is the person as interested in your values, lifestyle, and goals as he or she is in your financial situation?
3. Is he or she approachable, empathetic, a good communicator, and a good listener?
4. Is he or she willing to have regular meetings or conversations with you to make sure you're on track?
5. Does the person have a definite philosophy about building wealth?
6. Is the person willing to share his or her personal portfolio with you? In other words, does the person do for him- or herself what he or she advises others to do?
7. Does the person have specific experience with individuals planning retirement? What has his or her track record been with these clients? Can you interview a few of them?

Whether you use a financial adviser or do the numbers on your own, you may find—depending on your situation, the economy, and shifting societal attitudes—that you need to keep working longer than you had hoped. John, the health-care executive, is a good example of this. He has another six years to retirement and believes that planning for retirement is "like a chess game. It's important to position properly all the pieces of retirement—your 401(k), your pension if you have one, your IRA, medical insurance, your investments, and all the other financial tools that are relevant to your well-being." He goes on to say, "The other important part of thinking about retiring is 'where.' Where do you want to live?"

Choosing Where to Live When You're Retired

While a lower cost of living is important to many retirees, other reasons to move to a different location are for a better climate, community services geared toward the elderly, medical care, an easier lifestyle, a low crime rate, and a greater availability of property and land. The US Census Bureau projected that by the year 2020, Nevada, Arizona, Colorado, Utah, Washington, Georgia, Alaska, and California will double their older populations for many of these reasons. In addition, these states, plus Idaho and South Carolina, have seen an increase in older populations in the last ten years.

If you are considering moving to a different state, region, or another country, be sure to visit for a few weeks and talk to some of the residents, including people who have moved there to retire.

Another factor to consider when identifying where you'd like to retire is that retirees are moving to cities, rather than rural locations or planned adult fifty-five-and-older communities. In their early sixties, Jud and his wife, Chris, were feeling burned out from their job responsibilities and began to discuss the next phase in their lives. Unfortunately, they couldn't initially agree about what retirement would look like or where they would do it. The only location they agreed on was Providence, because they both had graduated from Brown University and liked the city's culture, diversity, and variety of restaurants. When Jud resigned from his senior executive role at a major university, his boss refused to accept his resignation, offering to rework Jud's responsibilities and location. So, the couple bought a twelve-room Victorian house (with a rental apartment!) in Providence, Rhode Island, and moved there from southern Connecticut. Jud and Chris plan on spending many years renovating every aspect of the house—from the plumbing to the exterior—while continuing to work in some way.

Here are some things you should look for when you're exploring a new geographic area to live.

- *Climate.* While warm weather may be appealing, can you handle suffocating summers? Some of the most popular states to which retirees move are South Dakota, North Dakota, Wyoming, Nebraska, and Iowa, despite their cold winters. On the other hand, it's generally less expensive to cool a house than to heat a house. And warm weather clothing is definitely cheaper.
- *Taxes.* What are the property taxes and state income and sales taxes? There are some states that do not tax Social Security. In 2014, some of the most tax-friendly states in the United States were Arizona, Delaware, Florida, Georgia, Louisiana, Mississippi, Nevada, and South Carolina.
- *Housing.* Are there specific types of houses that are appealing to you? Rental communities? Continuing-care housing? Shared housing?
- *Medical care.* Is there an adequate hospital? Are there enough doctors to take care of the community? Do you have a special health problem that can be monitored and taken care of?
- *Transportation.* Are there taxis and buses, and is there easy accessibility to the closest airport?
- *Proximity to your family and friends.* Is it easy to visit you? Is it a place that people will find appealing to visit?
- *Culture.* Are there museums, a theater, art galleries, a symphony? Are there libraries close by?
- *Social interactions.* Are there people in the community with similar cultural backgrounds or interests to whom you can relate?
- *Services for the elderly.* What kinds of community services exist for the aging?
- *Education.* Are there colleges or universities nearby where you can take classes?
- *Your interests.* Is this an area where you can involve yourself in your particular interest, such as art, music, fishing, hunting, skiing, tennis, or golf?

- *Industry.* What kinds of businesses exist? Are there companies where you can work full-time or part-time? Are there entrepreneurs who are starting new businesses and hiring employees?
- *Safety.* Is the crime rate low? Will you feel comfortable walking or driving around the area?
- *Economic confidence.* Does a long-term business and entrepreneurial growth pattern exist?
- *Affordability.* How much do food, gas, utilities, movie tickets, and clothing cost? How much does it cost to eat in a restaurant? What is the overall cost of living?

What Kind of Work Do You
Want to Do in Retirement?

The Futurist magazine predicts that "increasingly, over time, people will work at one career, 'retire' for a while when they can afford it, return to school, begin another career, and so on in endless variations. True retirement, a permanent end to work, will be delayed until very late in an extended life." Indeed, you may be part of the rapidly growing trend of older workers who are staying in the workforce. In some ways you are not unlike many of the people who fit into the other five situations in this book. Whether you are wondering, Where's the Meaning? or you are Bored and Plateaued, the first thing you must do is get reacquainted with yourself so that you can focus your goals and energy in the appropriate direction.

The Merrill Lynch report *Work in Retirement: Myths and Motivations* categorized people who are retired and work into four types:

- **Driven Achievers:** 15 percent of working retirees start "retire-preneurship" businesses, are extremely satisfied working, tend to be workaholics even in this stage of their life, and plan to work as long as possible.
- **Caring Contributors:** 33 percent of working older people fall into this category; they work for nonprofits (whether paid or unpaid),

are highly satisfied with work, and are motivated by giving back to their communities or worthwhile causes.

· **Life Balancers:** 24 percent of working retirees seek work that is fun and not stressful, and often work part-time; primarily they want to keep working to develop and maintain workplace friendships and social connections.

· **Earnest Earners:** 28 percent of working retirees need income in retirement to pay their bills, don't feel highly motivated, are less satisfied with working, and have many frustrations and regrets about working at this time in their life.

Take a moment and think about which one of the four types described in the Merrill Lynch study you may be.

As both a Life Balancer and a Caring Contributor, Jud, who moved with his wife to Providence at sixty-two, advises people who are thinking about their next phase to redefine their work portfolio early on. He plans on working in his current position in academia for another four to five years and then thinks he may start a landscape company, do some coaching, and sit on a board of directors. Jud has worked in advertising and human resources, started his own company, and is now in academia. His lifelong ability to seek out different work situations enables him to continually open the door to new opportunities.

Michael retired at age sixty-five and moved from New York City to Cape Cod, where he had owned a vacation home for years. He started helping a local florist part-time and now works three or four days a week delivering flowers. He tells stories about the times he rings someone's doorbell and the person opens the door to see Michael standing there with a bouquet of flowers. It gives him joy to see the delighted expression on that individual's face. He helps many elderly recipients of flowers find a vase, keeping them company for a few minutes. Michael, who worked as an executive in the outplacement business for many years, frankly never expected to get so much pleasure out of a task like delivering flowers, but he always knew that having meaning in his work was important. He is definitely a Life Balancer!

Have you always wanted to start your own business? Maybe you didn't think you could afford to or weren't willing to make the sacrifices when you were in your peak working years. Lee was reorganized out of a twenty-five-year career, and at fifty-seven, as he is eyeing retirement, he is on his own as a broker of award products for the incentive industry. He loves the independence and plans on dabbling in this business even when he slows down his work schedule.

Ernie enjoyed a very satisfying career as a product sales manager for a large chemical company. Over sixty, he officially retired from his job and immediately began pursuing opportunities to become a speaker with an emphasis on selling. In the beginning stages of his exploration of the speaking business, Ernie hired a coach to help him create a one-hour speech. Then he began learning more about the craft of speaking by joining Toastmasters (a national association that focuses on teaching people to speak) and several speakers' associations. He also started networking with his contacts in the chemical business to learn about possible speaking opportunities. While Ernie is excited about this new part-time "career," he also is adamant that his "basic thrust is to work at a level that will keep me interested and challenged, with the money being a secondary consideration."

What about simply working to fulfill some of your social needs or your desire to be useful, or to supplement your income? Zetta was ninety-four when she stopped working at the Top of the Falls souvenir shop in Niagara Falls, New York, during the peak tourist season, April to October. She had never had a steady career, opting instead to raise her three children full-time. On occasion she had worked as a jewelry engraver, an independent salesperson, a bank teller, and a clerical assistant. After not working for thirty years, Zetta took a job in the gift shop and worked there for more than twenty years. She explains that while she never got bored while home alone, she did get lonely, and truly enjoyed her interaction with the tourists. Zetta admitted that if she didn't have to show up for work, she wouldn't have stayed active. The best part? "I love meeting people. Sometimes I make an instant connection with someone, and even if I know I will never see the person again, I feel as if I have a friend for life." Zetta taught herself German using audiotapes and videotapes and had fun trying to talk to the many German-speaking tourists who visited Niagara Falls. She made $8.25 an hour, which supplemented her Social Security. While the small amount of money helped, the other benefits far outweighed the financial ones. The only reason she stopped working at the gift shop was because she could no longer drive herself to and from work.

Corporations are learning that retaining, retraining, and hiring older workers is a smart business strategy. In an era in which the ability to find workers with the right skills has become more difficult for companies, the older worker is often the solution to this problem. In addition to the marketplace's need for talented labor and a greater availability of people in older age groups, there are other reasons that make it sensible to hire older workers:

• Bringing back people who had worked at a corporation previously helps preserve the corporate memory, a crucial component of a corporate culture.

• Rapid changes in the job market and technology have necessitated the need for additional education and retraining for every level of employee. More and more, even small companies see this as a necessary investment rather than an expense. Also, the traditional bias toward training only new employees or senior managers appears to be diminishing. This creates a willingness to hire the older worker and to train him or her alongside everyone else.

• There are employers who are creating programs specifically to recruit and retain older workers because of their knowledge, experience, and work ethic, according to a *New York Times* article called "The Age Premium: Retaining Older Workers." CVS offers a "snowbird" program in which several hundred pharmacists and other employees are transferred from stores in northern states during the winter to pharmacies in Florida and other warm states. The National Institutes of Health (NIH), a federal agency, offers emergency care for employees' parents. In 2014, the NIH reported that 48 percent of their almost twenty thousand employees are over the age of fifty. Home Depot is known for hiring thousands of older workers; many of them are retired plumbers and contractors, eager to take part-time jobs there.

Melody has had a successful career as an insurance underwriter and loved the technical aspects of her work, and, like many of us, Melody has suffered through many less than enjoyable work situations. A year or so after her husband retired, Melody found herself in yet another difficult and stressful work environment and decided to retire to keep her husband company as well as to restore her psychological well-being. She stopped working, traveled, read, and caught up on projects she hadn't been able to do while working. The first year or so was great, but Melody, only in her early fifties, began to feel antsy. While she did retire at an earlier age than most people do, she feels that if she had put more time into planning her retirement, she would have experienced more satisfaction. She went back to work, but in a job that was at a much lower level than any of her previous positions, and while the challenge and the status no longer existed, the long hours and demands on her were still there. On top of this, her compensation was much reduced from her previous employment as an underwriter. She eventually left that job and at fifty-five took a job comparable to the one she had left before she retired. She plans to retire again when it makes sense, but this time she says her approach will be different. She will spend more time preparing herself mentally and will organize her affairs before she actually retires. Her advice? "Take the time to plan your retirement. It should be approached just like a job search. If you don't, you may be shocked by what you'll experience when you retire."

Step 3: Create an Action Plan

It is nice to know that as you are approaching retirement, you have a wide array of options available to you. Whether you are champing at the bit to retire and never work again (15 percent of people planning retirement don't want to work at all) or excited about start-ing a second part-time career, there are some things you should think about and do before you take the plunge. Examine the details of your life as if you are doing "due diligence" to buy a business:

• All of the many financial details that are so important to your retirement should be scrutinized and analyzed by you and by experts.

• Make sure you are debt-free by prioritizing paying off outstand-ing balances on credit cards, installment loans, car loans, and even your mortgage.

• Look for ways to trim your living expenses.

• If you can, wait as long as possible to collect your Social Security benefits so that you will receive the maximum amount for which you are eligible. Payments are reduced if you sign up before your full retirement age, which is typically sixty-six or sixty-seven, depend-ing upon your birth year. Monthly payments also increase for each additional year you delay claiming, up to age seventy.

• Allow yourself to dream about the different work opportunities you can explore. Whether you want to start a business, hang out a consult-ing shingle, or work part-time for a company, you can believe that anything is possible. Does the world discriminate against older people in the workforce? Of course. Your objective, however, is to find that niche for yourself where discrimination won't affect you. In "The Best Jobs for Retirees" on Investopedia.com, some areas are described as ideally suited for older workers, including: consulting; craftsmanship (calligraphy, artwork, candle making, cabinetry); entrepreneurship; working online as a virtual assistant; editing; tutoring; telemarketing; retail sales; and teaching an adult education class at parks and recre-ation centers or by giving webinars. Other job opportunities exist in food service, health care, child and pet care, and customer service.

• Do much of the legwork and planning for your new work ven-ture *before* you retire. Give yourself a reasonable amount of time to learn about what you need to know and do.

• Check out RetireOnYourTerms.org for a lot of helpful advice, a newsletter and articles, and an active social media presence.

• Get a clean bill of health. Make appointments with all your doctors, including your internist, dentist, dermatologist, and any other specialists.

Use the following questions to plan your retirement:

1. Do you have a financial adviser with whom you feel comfortable?

   _____

2. If not, when will you begin getting referrals and interviewing advisers?

   _____

   _____

3. Are there geographic locations to which you are interested in relocating? What are they?

   _____

   _____

   _____

   _____

4. Have you investigated them thoroughly? If not, when do you plan to do so?

   _____

   _____

5. If you are working now, when do you plan to leave your job?

   _____

   _____

6. Have you thought about the kind of work you'd like to do when you leave your current position? If so, what is it? Check out RetirementJobs.com, which offers job listings and career advice for people over fifty, or Encore.org, which coordinates a network of organizations offering a fellowship program for people, many whom average twenty-five years of work experience.

   _____

   _____

   _____

   _____

7. What steps do you plan on taking to create new work or find your next job?

   _____

   _____

   _____

   _____

Remember that this next phase in your life should be fun, interesting, fulfilling, illuminating, and exhilarating! In an article written by Lydia Bronte, who was a senior fellow at the Hunter College Brookdale Center on Aging before she passed away in 2003, commented, "Some people find their best fit careerwise after the age of fifty and some, even more surprisingly, after the age of sixty-five.

People need to keep in mind that the best part of your career may still be ahead of you."

Jerry is a great example of this. After working in multiple careers that included the navy, consumer product sales, executive search and outplacement, Jerry, at sixty-eight, is retired from the corporate world. He started his own small company, which provides career transition seminars for flag-rank military (admirals and generals), counseling and retention classes at the US Naval War College in Newport, Rhode Island, and other career management services for junior naval officers. He feels so blessed that at the end of a series of successful careers, he has been able to create work for himself that he loves and excels at. Jerry says, "I feel that my background in management as well as the need to 'do good' have prepared me for the work I'm doing, which has real meaning. I'm away from corporate politics, although I miss the social interaction. As long as God gives me the health and the credibility, I plan on continuing to contribute as long as possible, perhaps ratcheting down a bit at a time. This year I'll work about ten percent less than last year, but I get paid real well for what I do, and I have a modest Navy Reserve retirement and also now collect Social Security."

Joanie is another great example of this. You first met Joanie in chapter 1 as someone whose manager openly discriminated against her when she turned fifty. When Joanie was fifty-two, both her longtime partner and her father died, and she left her lucrative job and moved to southern Florida to be near her mom. Joanie took a few months off and then dabbled in many jobs, including real estate, recruiting, working with a developer, and temp positions. She fell in love (again!) and married, and finally, in her early sixties, Joanie took an administrative job at an engineering firm. She has great benefits and likes to say that she spends most of her day laughing in a rather carefree environment.

Joanie says, "I am very happy; my job allows me the freedom to be with my husband stress-free and spend time with my ninety-six-year-old (going on fifty-six) mom. My husband and I decided that we would prefer less pressure and less income, and we have a simple, albeit wonderful, life together."

Joanie has been with the engineering firm for five years, and last year reduced her hours to thirty-four a week, with Fridays off. She has some time for herself on the weekend, and she spends one day every weekend with her mom. Joanie plans to stay with this company till she is sixty-nine and then will finally "retire."

Stanford University's Distinguished Careers Institute launched in 2015 the first yearlong program for twenty high-achieving individuals with twenty- to thirty-year career histories who were ready to explore new career trajectories. Institute director Dr. Phil Pizzo, a sixty-nine-year-old pediatrician and former dean of Stanford School of Medicine, believes, "Retirement in the traditional sense is not really healthy. What you need to stay healthy is to be physically well, intellectually motivated and stimulated to take on new challenges, and involved with social communities," he said, "and to continue to do that over time."

Retirement can and should be an interesting and fulfilling phase in your life. It is an ideal time to experiment with different kinds of work without the stress and pressures that you may have experienced in your career. As an AARP ad says, "Age is just a number, and life is what you make of it."

CHAPTER 11

The Eleven Keys to Success

In his bestselling book *Emotional Intelligence*, Daniel Goleman writes, "There are widespread exceptions to the myth that IQ predicts success. . . . At best, IQ contributes about 20 percent to the factors that determine life success, which leaves 80 percent to other forces." Goleman goes on to explain, "These 'other characteristics' are called *emotional intelligence*: abilities such as being able to motivate oneself and persist in the face of frustrations; to control impulse and delay gratification; to regulate one's moods and keep distress from swamping the ability to think; to empathize and to hope."

This book is full of assessments, tools, resources, and how-tos to help guide you in finding new work that will better meet your personal and financial needs. No matter which category you fit within, however, unless you are able to demonstrate and master a very specific set of life skills and traits, you will find it very difficult to be successful in finding the work you want.

"The Eleven Keys to Success" come from intuitive observations of and experience with people in the workplace. Time and again it is apparent that those individuals who exhibit these eleven keys and use them most productively are consistently the more successful and well-liked individuals overall. The good news is that most people are born with at least some of these keys or learned them at a very young age, and all of these keys can be developed or learned later in life.

These are the Eleven Keys to Success:

1. **Confidence:** an unshakable belief in oneself based on a realistic understanding of one's circumstances; a trait that most people admire in others and strive to acquire themselves.

2. **Curiosity:** being eager to know and learn; always being the person who says, "I want to know more about . . ."; always showing interest and giving special attention to the less obvious.

3. **Decisiveness:** arriving at a final conclusion or making a choice and taking action; making decisions with determination even when you don't have all the information you think you need.

4. **Empathy:** demonstrating caring and understanding of someone else's situation, feelings, and motives; always thinking about what it's like to walk in someone else's shoes.

5. **Flexibility:** being capable of change; responding positively to change; being pliable, adaptable, non-rigid, and able to deal with ambiguity.

6. **Humor:** viewing yourself and the world with enjoyment; not taking life or yourself too seriously; being amusing, amused, and, at times, even comical.

7. **Intelligence:** thinking and working smartly and cleverly; being sharp in your dealings; "not reinventing the wheel"; planning before acting; working efficiently and focusing on quality over quantity. (Important note: This is different from IQ, the common abbreviation for intelligence quotient.)

8. **Optimism:** expecting the best possible outcome and dwelling on the most hopeful or positive aspects of a situation; subscribing to the belief that "the glass is half full" rather than "half empty."

9. **Perseverance:** having passion, energy, focus, and the desire to get results; motivation, persistence, and hard work.
10. **Respect:** remembering that it is just as easy to be nice; protecting another person's self-esteem; treating others in a considerate and courteous manner.
11. **Self-awareness:** a sophisticated form of consciousness that enables you to regulate yourself by self-monitoring, observing yourself, and changing your thought processes and behaviors.

Which of these keys are among your strengths? Which of the eleven are among your weaknesses? Self-awareness, the eleventh key, is really the foundation for understanding yourself. If you are not sure how self-aware you are, ask several people whom you trust which of these eleven keys they believe are your strengths and which are not. Again, while no one person possesses all eleven of these keys in equal amounts, each of them can be developed and improved.

Confidence

Self-confidence—an unshakable belief in oneself based on a realistic understanding of one's circumstances—is a trait that most people admire in others and strive to acquire themselves. Confident people exude positive energy that draws others to them like a magnet. They tend to be optimists and risk takers, and they excel at working under pressure, tolerating frustration, and coping with adversity. Confident individuals usually appear calm, relaxed, and "comfortable in their own skin." These are the people we all want to work with because their confidence is inspiring and becomes contagious.

It is important to possess a healthy level of confidence in order to change your career, start a business, or look for a job. A large part of the process for any of these changes seems ambiguous and uncertain; therefore, keeping your perspective at a realistic level is a must!

Assess Your Confidence

Take the following assessment to help you decide whether you lack confidence, have too much confidence, or have just the right amount.

Indicate how true each statement is for you by placing the appropriate number in the blank to the left of the statement.

5 = Definitely true
4 = Often true
3 = Somewhat true
2 = Rarely true
1 = Almost never true

____ 1. I really like and accept who I am.

____ 2. Usually I do not take mistakes or setbacks personally and can view them as learning experiences.

____ 3. I never spend time thinking about how I can avoid looking bad or being embarrassed.

____ 4. I believe that I deserve the best that life has to offer.

____ 5. I can easily make a list of eight accomplishments in my work and personal life in the last five years.

____ 6. I express my opinions and feelings openly.

____ 7. I really trust my intuition or "gut" and follow what it tells me.

____ 8. I am able to visualize what I want or need and make it happen.

____ 9. I feel proud of myself when I overcome obstacles or improve something about myself.

___10. I am always conscious of how important my image (that is, demeanor, appearance, the way you act and communicate) is.

___11. I accept compliments graciously and without discomfort.

___12. I enjoy feeling successful.

___13. I have no trouble saying no to other people when I need to.

____ 14. I don't believe that others' perceptions of me are more accurate than my own.

____ 15. I do not need to be liked by everyone in my life at all times.

____ 16. My past does not influence my behavior and feelings.

____ 17. I don't often magnify the negative aspects of things.

____ 18. My behavior almost always reflects the way I feel inside.

SCORE KEY

Add up the numbers that you entered for each question. If you scored:

18 to 35	Your low self-confidence is probably negatively affecting many aspects of your life. It may make sense to seek professional counseling to understand why your self-assurance is so low.
36 to 54	You probably feel confidence in some areas of your life and less confidence in others. While this is normal for many people, it could benefit you to focus on increasing your confidence in those areas that can use it.
55 to 72	You like and respect yourself and have learned to accept both your positive and negative qualities. Because you feel good about yourself, you tend to enjoy life.
73 to 90	You may be too confident at times and not have a realistic outlook of yourself. People could view you as egotistical or conceited at times. It is possible that you aren't actually that confident but cover it up by acting overly confident.

If your score fell between 55 and 72 and you feel comfortable with your level of confidence, you may want to focus on how to deal with other people who are either too confident or are not confident enough.

If you scored lower than you would like or fell into the too-confident category, the following assessments will help you pinpoint some reasons and the behaviors you exhibit.

If you would like to boost your confidence, try one of the following exercises:

Give Yourself Credit for Past Effort and Successes

Write down two positive things that you have achieved in the last six months. Have you learned something new? Have you started an exercise program or lost weight? Have you solved a problem that had been bugging you?

_____

_____

_____

Now think about what you did to make your accomplishment happen. Did you adjust your attitude? Did you write down your goal and look at it frequently? Did you take a class, read a book, or ask someone for help?

_____

_____

_____

_____

The purpose of this exercise is to remind you that you have recently been successful in making something good happen for yourself, and if you've done it before, you can do it again. Applauding yourself for achieving something meaningful or desirable to you, no matter how simple, is a great technique for developing confidence.

Create a Positive "Incantation"

If you lack confidence, you may have a habit of using negative "self-talk," unflattering or overly critical words that you say to yourself either silently or out loud and that only make you feel less confident. An incantation is a simple phrase or group of words recited to produce a magical effect. In this case the desired magical effect is bolstering your self-image. To help create your incantation, write down something negative that you habitually say about yourself, either out loud or silently. Here's an example: Whenever Gwen forgets to ask her boss a question, she always tells herself, "I did something really stupid." If Gwen took time to think about it logically, she would realize that the idea of labeling herself "stupid" just because she didn't get all the information she needs from her boss is, well, ridiculous!

Now think of a positive phrase or motivating expression that has meaning to you and write it down. In Gwen's case she might write, "Create an opportunity to connect." The next time Gwen forgets to ask her boss something, she can say to herself, "I just created another opportunity to connect with my boss!"

_____

_____

The next time you catch yourself using negative self-talk, quickly substitute the incantation you've just written down. Doing this repeatedly will help you develop belief in yourself, and create a new habit of positive self-talk. Gradually, this new habit will replace your old one and help you strengthen your faith in yourself.

Take a Risk

People with low confidence tend to shy away from undertaking new experiences because of their fear of failure. Learning to approach new experiences as opportunities to learn new things, rather than occasions to win or lose, is the key to positive risk taking. Think of something at work you'd like to do, something that you see as risky (which has prevented you from doing it). Do you want to network with a senior executive in your company? Do you want to volunteer for a task force? Do you want to make a presentation at an upcoming meeting? Whatever it is, write it down.

_____

_____

_____

Write down, step-by-step, what you have to do to make that thing you're itching to do—but are afraid of—happen. Try to keep it simple. Do you need to learn more about the thing you have in mind? Who do you need to talk with? What kind of preparation do you need to do? What about taking a class?

_____

_____

_____

_____

Now that you've named the risky thing you'd like to do and the steps needed to accomplish it, write down the three worst things that might happen if you take a risk and fail to achieve the results you were hoping for.

_____

_____

_____

Realistically, what are the chances of each one of these things happening? If it did happen, how would you, or someone you care about, be affected? Now look at your answers and try to honestly determine how much they are based on your fear or on a logical assessment of the situation.

What Do You Like About Yourself?

Make a list of five things you like about yourself. Don't ask anyone else what he or she likes about you. Make this list on your own.

_____

_____

_____

What Do Other People Like About You?

Ask five people to tell you one thing that they like about you. If someone repeats an answer you've already received, ask for a different answer. Write the answers down.

_____

_____

_____

_____

Are any of the answers the same as yours? If so, that's great because it confirms that what you already know about yourself is what others value about you as well. Now write the entire list on an index card or put it into your smartphone. Whenever you are feeling less confident, go to a place where you have some privacy, pull out your list, and read it aloud!

Healthy confidence is one of the most valuable assets you can have in life and in a job search or career change. Of the Eleven Keys, confidence is one of the hardest keys to learn and maintain, but without it the other keys can't be learned as easily.

Curiosity

Are you curious? Do you constantly seek to learn about new ideas and gather additional information, no matter what the topic? Or are you concerned only with learning about and knowing just what interests you? When you meet a new person, do you really make an effort to get to know him or her, or are many of your encounters superficial in nature?

We all have an unlimited potential for learning. We can also hold ourselves back from learning by allowing certain fears, such as a fear of failure or a fear of success, to inhibit us. Sometimes we let a lack of training or experience keep us from being inquisitive and interested in new things. The trouble with this approach is that being curious and learning about people, jobs, and business are extremely necessary to the process of finding satisfying work. Our natural tendency is to believe that we must be interested in something before we are willing to learn more about it. Yet at times we surprise ourselves by becoming interested in something we didn't think we cared about.

Jonathan had the courage to leave a secure job at a Fortune 50 company in order to seek a more rewarding and challenging career and to balance his family life, which included his newborn daughter. He hired a career counselor who helped him define his unique strengths, skills, passions, and hidden talents. He honed his curiosity by networking in diverse areas of business, attending trade shows, and exploring fields he had never been exposed to directly. Jonathan read books, listened to audiobooks, and attended presentations about career change. All of the information he absorbed really opened his eyes to the career possibilities that existed for him. He started his own company doing business strategy and due diligence, and he leads a very balanced life that includes participating in his daughter's life and spending time on his boat, things he would never be able to do if he still worked for the Fortune 50 company.

When you are curious and interested in learning from others, it shows. Constantly asking questions of the people you meet and really listening to their answers during the process of exploring new career situations and opportunities—as well as in your other social interactions, both formal and informal—are great ways to develop your curiosity. Becoming a better listener will help you become more curious and interested. Really focusing intently on what people are saying, without jumping to immediate conclusions, will enable you to learn and understand information more easily. Trying to understand and learn about people's motives, feelings, and emotions—not just facts—is important as well.

Decisiveness

Making decisions is a crucial part of changing your work. One of the reasons so many people remain in an unhappy or unsatisfying job situation is that they simply can't make any decisions. The trouble with this is that without decisions there are no results! Decisions are based on gathering as much information as possible without getting stuck in a state of "analysis paralysis." Involving the people who are affected by your decisions, such as your advisers or your family, is also a meaningful part of making decisions. Your intuition—that is, what your "gut," "inner voice," or "sixth sense" tells you to do—is another significant element of decision making. Balancing these three components can be a challenge, and making a decision, let alone making the one that's best for you, is often not that simple.

It is also very important to remember that there is no perfect decision. Deciding finally to do something about being unhappy with your work is one of the hardest decisions you can make in life. But once you have done so, continuing to make small decisions along the way will not only become easier but will also help you feel better.

If you can't make a decision easily, ask yourself what the worst possible outcome could be. Rarely does the worst possible scenario ever happen, but even if it does, ask yourself what you would do if it did and how you could turn it around.

How can you be more decisive? If you follow this simple thought process when making a decision, it will become much easier:

1. Define a specific problem or situation with your work. Try to focus on the actual problem, not the symptoms.
2. Decide what it is that you want to achieve. In other words, what do you want the immediate outcome of your decision to be? What about the long-term outcome?

3. Consider your options.
4. Do you have all the information you need to make the decision? If not, and the information is accessible, obtaining the information will make the decision a lot easier for you. You can use the formula that journalists use by asking yourself: Who? What? Where? When? Why? How? If you have all this information, there should be no reason not to make the decision.
5. Do you have to make this decision alone? While so much of the process of finding satisfying work comes from you, there is no need to do it alone. Consult with people who are supportive of you and those who are experts or at least knowledgeable about you and your situation.
6. How have you handled similar issues in the past? If you haven't had to make decisions related to your career in the past, find out how other people have done so. It is time to learn how to make this an easier and more comfortable process.
7. Do you have a track record of making poor decisions? If so, why? Is there something you can change about how you make decisions?
8. Do you rely too heavily on other people's input? Everyone has an opinion, whether you ask for it or not. Sift through this information and use what makes sense for you.
9. Is there someone whose style of decision making you admire? Are you able to spend some time with that person to learn how he or she makes decisions?
10. If you had to decide quickly, what would your immediate decision be about what to do next regarding your career?

In making decisions, be willing to take risks and to forgive yourself if you make a decision that doesn't turn out to be the right one for you.

Darleen started a candy business with her husband, and after working in the business for five years—every one of which was miserable—she admitted that opening the business was a mistake. Once she faced the fact that the decision to operate the candy business wasn't a good one, she made another decision: to cut her losses. She sold the candy business and started a technology training business. Running the candy business had been a painful experience, and unfortunately it took Darleen a long time to decide to close it and start a different type of business. But she did make a change and has never been happier.

Gene left a successful career in the construction business to go to law school. With a wife and three children to consider, he was not sure how he would make it work. When he was thinking about taking the plunge, he said, "At some point I realized that the *only* thing that stood between me and a law degree was simply the decision to do it." When Gene described his decision-making process, he said, "I like to make decisions that have inherent guarantees of success. That does not mean risk is to be avoided. To the contrary, you can embrace risk if you focus your energy on breaking down any barriers to success. In the decision-making process that I engaged in, I simply identified all the barriers and then sought a way to overcome each barrier."

Empathy

According to Daniel Goleman, empathy builds on self-awareness. This means that the more in tune we are with ourselves and our emotions, the more skilled we will be in reading someone else's feelings. Your capacity or ability to know or intuit how someone else feels is key to successful interactions with others in your career-discovery process. Goleman says, "The key to intuiting another's feelings is in the ability to read nonverbal channels: tone of voice, gesture, facial expression, and the like." He goes on to say that "the benefits of being able to read feelings from nonverbal cues include being better adjusted emotionally, more popular, more outgoing, and—perhaps not surprisingly—more sensitive." Your ability to understand and read other people will greatly increase your comfort level with the process of discovering work that will fulfill your needs. Being empathetic toward others will sharpen your insights about what makes people thrive and be happy in their work. You can then more easily relate these insights to your own needs and desires regarding finding new work.

There are several simple things you can do to enhance your empathy toward others:

- Ask questions and really listen to the answers.
- Respond to the answers with additional well-thought-out questions.
- Respond to body language, facial expressions, and eye contact.
- Try to understand what other people are thinking and feeling, and what may be motivating them.
- Whenever you start thinking about yourself, immediately refocus your attention on the other person.

Jonathan, who left the Fortune 50 company to search for a new career, didn't focus on his own needs. When he realized how challenging and emotionally charged a job search can be, he started investing his time in meeting and coaching other unemployed individuals. He found that by volunteering his time to offer advice and hope to others, he became more empathetic in his own career quest. As he found himself becoming more interested in other people and less focused on himself, his interactions with other people were more meaningful during his job search.

Flexibility

It can be rather difficult to pursue a new career or a new type of work without being flexible. You may prefer more structure, and as a result, you may favor following a routine that enables you to know where you will be and what you will be doing most of the time. Unfortunately, such a predictable lifestyle is difficult to achieve through the many phases of looking for gratifying work.

During this process you will be initiating conversations and having meetings with people you have never met before or don't know well. Any of these individuals may give you a new or different idea or piece of information that could be very useful to you. Being open to the unexpected is important. Saying such things as "I would never do that" will make you appear rigid to other people and could deter them from offering you helpful information.

The quest for new work usually presents constant change and ambiguity. Learning to cope with these challenges can be difficult; however, if you choose not to deal with them in a positive way or to completely resist them, you will find that your attitude will negatively affect other people's perceptions of you.

Maria, the self-employed ESL instructor and consultant, admits that she is not very flexible emotionally. Although she is constantly seeking the new, the unknown, and the next challenge, at the same time she loves the comfort of the secure and the predictable. This presents a true conflict for Maria. The way she deals with this conflict is by automatically asking herself if she is being flexible in her approach, communication, and attitude.

Humor

Humor can relieve the stress of the seemingly monumental process you are thinking of undertaking. There are so many times, situations, and circumstances during your search for gratifying work when a chuckle or a good laugh is all you need to shift your mood or change your outlook from negative to positive.

Daniel Goleman explains that happiness can actually cause physiological changes in the human brain as well as in our overall physical and psychological well-being. Happiness, he says, can bring about "an increased activity that inhibits negative feelings and fosters an increase in available energy, and a quieting of those feelings that generate worrisome thought. This configuration offers the body a general rest, as well as readiness and enthusiasm for whatever task is at hand and for striving toward a variety of goals."

A scientific explanation for this phenomenon is that laughter, which typically results from humor, stimulates endorphins in the brain, which in turn decreases physical or emotional pain. It is hoped that you won't experience too much—or any—pain during this process! At times, though, you will feel discomfort, uneasiness, or other unpleasant emotions that humor and its by-product—laughter—will relieve.

How can you generate and sustain humor?

- Keep a progressive record of your career-search journey, writing down the humorous moments that occur.
- If you are experiencing stress, learn to view your experiences from an amusing perspective.
- Nurture your sense of humor by going to a comedy club, renting funny movies, and reading humorous books.
- Try to surround yourself with upbeat, smiling, happy, and lighthearted individuals. Humor is contagious!

Intelligence

Intelligence is about thinking and working smart, realizing where your intelligence lies, and taking advantage of other people's intelligence as well. While your specific career situation is very personal, remember that there are innumerable people in the world who have already experienced the same things you are going through. These people have created new work, changed careers, started and bought businesses, and accomplished everything that is discussed in this book. Intelligence is finding a handful of people who have been in the same boat and learning from their mistakes and successes.

Christina is in her late thirties and has changed careers four times already. She worked in investment banking and then became an independent event planner. After that she worked as an independent contractor, before moving into her current job running the North American operation of a global network of health managers. When asked for an example of how she demonstrated intelligence in her career changing, she said, "It is very important to develop or improve skills that you will need during the process of changing careers. At the same time, I believe that we are all good at many things and less good at other things, and we shouldn't waste our time pulling energy away from the good stuff, especially since the 'good stuff' is usually what we like best anyway."

This means that if it isn't fun or productive to reinvent the wheel while moving through the process of reshaping your work, find someone who already has and ask that person to share his or her findings with you.

Optimism

This particular quality gets a lot of attention in the world today, and deservedly so! If I had to choose three keys of the eleven that are the most basic to your success in the pursuit of satisfying work, I'd say that optimism is one of them, the other two being perseverance and curiosity. Motivational speaker Keith Harrell believes that "attitude is everything, and life is not what happens to you, it's what you do about it."

Martin Seligman, PhD, the author of *Learned Optimism*, says, "Optimistic people feel that good things will last a long time and will have a beneficial effect on everything they do. They think that bad things are isolated: They won't last too long and won't affect other parts of life."

Seligman says, "Positive thinkers feel powerful, and negative thinkers feel helpless because they have been conditioned to believe that they're screwed no matter what."

Take this brief quiz to see how you score as a positive person. Circle the answer that most describes you.

1. You arrive at the airport only to find out you've missed your flight because your car service was twenty minutes late picking you up and you hit traffic on the way.
   A. You yell at the ticket agent and demand that he get you on the next flight *and* put you in business class.
   B. You politely inquire which flight is the next one to leave and then smile and say, "I had a few phone calls to make anyway."
2. You're about to give a major presentation to some senior executives at your company, and five minutes before you're scheduled to start, you can't get the LCD projector to turn on.
   A. You mutter loudly under your breath, "Goddammit, this always happens to me. When is technology ever going to work?"
   B. You announce to the group that you really think that your presentation has more impact without the Power-Point slides and plan to begin in two minutes if everyone is ready.
3. Your boss sits down with you and tells you that he's very sorry but he is going to have to let you go as part of a big organizational budget-cutting initiative.
   A. You react angrily and tell him that you'll never find another job at your same level of compensation and hope he feels good about ruining your career.
   B. You take a deep breath and say, "Well, this is a bit of a shock, so when I feel calmer, I'd like to meet with you to discuss arrangements for my separation package."
4. You have finally decided to explore a new field after taking some diagnostic tests and doing research. During your first networking meeting, the person you are talking to casually mentions that it's a tough field to break into.

    A. You go home and tell your spouse that you'll never get hired in the new industry and maybe you'd better just look for another job in your current field.

    B. You ask your networking contact what advice she would give you about the things you can do to ease your entry into the field.

5. You've been recruiting and interviewing candidates for three months for a key position in your department. You finally find the ideal candidate, and just as you're about to make her an offer, your boss tells you that he's decided not to increase the head count in your department for this fiscal year.

    A. Frustrated, you become emotional and tell your boss that he's making your job impossible to do and that you'll never hit your business goals without this new person on board.

    B. You ask your boss if you can sit down with him and have a planning meeting about ways that you can utilize other resources within your company to help you accomplish your objectives for the year. You also make an effort to stay in touch with the candidates in the hope that eventually the head count situation will turn around.

SCORE KEY

Needless to say, if you did (or really wanted to) select any "A" answers, these are not the approaches an optimist would take.

Optimism is said to be genetically predisposed; however, research has shown that environment and life experiences have just as much to do with one's tendency toward optimism. It has been proven, too, that optimism can be learned.

How can you become more optimistic?

- Whenever something negative or difficult happens, ask yourself what you've learned from your experience. Write this down so that the next time something similar happens, you're better prepared to handle it.

- If you are thinking about something in a negative way, distract yourself immediately by remembering an incident that made you laugh recently or by thinking about how you can relax over the weekend.
- It is easy to be negative if you're feeling overwhelmed. The best way to stop feeling overwhelmed is to think of everything in small steps and little pieces. What is the one thing you can do today to move toward accomplishing your goals?
- Immediately call or e-mail the most positive person you know and ask him or her to help you reframe your negative thoughts.
- Exercise. Get some fresh air. Try a new yoga class. Do something—anything—physical to change your perspective and get those endorphins flowing! The Mayo Clinic conducted a study that compared the health of more than eight hundred men and women to their scores on a personality test they had taken thirty years earlier. Those individuals who tested high on the optimism scale years ago were 19 percent more likely to be alive than their less optimistic fellow test takers.
- Focus on the positive aspects of your life, no matter how small: the clean bill of health you recently received from your doctor, your new haircut, the golf outing you have planned with your buddies, the big bouquet of tulips you bought for yourself, or the e-mail you just received from your old college friend.

Perseverance

Steve Mariucci, the former National Football League coach, said, "I never wear a watch, because I always know it's now—and now is when you should do it."

Without perseverance you will not achieve at the highest levels. It is necessary for goal setting, learning, developing and nurturing

227

relationships, and maintaining momentum. Changing careers requires an extraordinary amount of energy and motivation, and perseverance encompasses these two things as well as focus and the desire for results. For the most part, motivation comes from inside yourself: your thoughts, your behavior, and your attitudes.

Maria received her master's degree in teaching English as a second language at the age of fifty-four. She had always gravitated toward business situations that were new and not established and believes that "drive pushes us toward uncharted territory, but eventually we decide to stop and develop what we've learned into something." In Maria's case, she designed a program for Japanese nationals on how to live and conduct business when they are sent to the United States as staff for American branches of Japanese companies. Without perseverance, Maria would not have been able to make a success of her new business. She was motivated, focused, and passionate about learning what the Japanese nationals needed, and created the right program.

How can you develop perseverance? The first step is to feel passionate about your goals, about the career you have or the one you are trying to move into. Passion is very personal, and you will feel it only if what you are investigating and moving toward is right for you. If you are pursuing someone else's idea of what you should be doing, it will be nearly impossible for you to feel passionate.

Setting very specific activity goals during every phase of your search for satisfying work is a must, even for the introspective and soul-searching phase. Goals represent your purpose and the outcome you wish to achieve. Even the most motivated person will lag in his or her efforts at times without goals to work toward. Keep your goals simple, measurable, and realistic.

Find someone else who is going through a similar situation with his or her work, and agree to partner with this person in your individual searches for new work. Set up a healthy but competitive relationship to compare notes and coach each other along toward accomplishing your goals. The goals you might set for each other could include completing research on a specific industry by a specific deadline and scheduling a specific number of informational meetings. When you are held accountable in this friendly yet competitive way, you will be motivated much more than if you set goals on your own and share them with no one.

Without physical energy you will be unable to maintain a high level of motivation for long. Keep your energy level high by staying healthy, working out, and eating properly. Take time off regularly during your quest for new and satisfying work and keep your mental, emotional, and spiritual health intact. Hire a feng shui expert or an organizational consultant to help you streamline or reorganize your work environment. Think of statements or phrases that you can say to yourself to motivate you when you aren't feeling positive or focused—such as "All I need to do to keep going is . . ." or "I can do this."

Stefanie, an independent consultant in private practice with her husband, says after having several successful careers as a psychologist, the manager of an outplacement office, and an entrepreneur, "I have huge respect for perseverance as a quality." She knows that "talent goes nowhere without perseverance. It has been a key ingredient in my career. I had the perseverance to get my PhD and to get licensed; to get promoted to run an office; to run a successful and profitable office for my employer; and to run a successful consulting practice as an entrepreneur."

Respect

My father was fond of saying, "It's just as easy to be nice." Being pleasant and gracious to everyone without exception, using good manners by always saying "Please," "Thank you," and "Excuse me," and complimenting others so they feel good about themselves are all the basics of respect. So are appreciating differences in others, being honest, listening, keeping your word, and not blaming others when something goes wrong.

You may be thinking, "Isn't this pretty obvious stuff?" Well, yes, it should be; however, we all know people who don't routinely exhibit respectful behavior to others.

The Walt Disney Company, Southwest Airlines, and Four Seasons are three companies that look for civility when they interview applicants. A *Harvard Business Review* article titled "The Price of Incivility" examined rudeness at work and determined that there are tangible costs of incivility, including decreased productivity, declined performance, a lessened commitment to the organization, increased stress, and other negative repercussions.

In your interactions with other people during the course of your pursuit for fulfilling work, being conscious of how considerate you are will improve your overall success. People want to help individuals who are polite, gracious and appreciative, not those who don't exhibit these behaviors.

Self-awareness

Self-awareness may well be the most complex of the Eleven Keys for two reasons: because of what it involves and because it's more difficult to develop. It involves knowing and understanding aspects of yourself and their relations to other people; the meaning of your appraisals and actions; your wants, intentions, and goals; and your attitudes, hopes, and fears. Without self-awareness it is nearly impossible to develop a balanced level of any of the other keys. In other words, self-awareness is at the core of balancing confidence, curiosity, decisiveness, empathy, flexibility, humor, intelligence, optimism, perseverance, and respect. On the other hand, having a high level of self-awareness does not guarantee that you will automatically command just the right amount of the other keys if you are not motivated to do so.

Self-awareness is a sophisticated form of consciousness that enables you to become the object of your own attention by being aware of your perceptions, sensations, attitudes, intentions, and emotions as well as your behaviors and general physical appearance. It is fundamentally important to possess self-awareness because it enables you to regulate yourself by self-monitoring, observing yourself, and changing your thought processes and behaviors.

The three primary sources of self-awareness are the social environment, the physical world, and one's self. The social world involves receiving verbal and nonverbal feedback from other people and deciding how relevant it is. The social environment also presents opportunities to make comparisons between yourself and others, which increases self-awareness. The physical world provides stimuli that generate self-awareness such as cameras, mirrors, recordings of your voice, newspapers, reality TV, movies, and the Internet. The third source of self-awareness is your own self, which generates self-talk, imagery, and mental and physical awareness.

Here are some exercises and activities that will help you become more self-aware.

Be Curious About Yourself

Most people tend to become either more or less curious with age. When they reach middle age, some people can become set in their ways and stop trying to understand how they come across to others. In all fairness, young people can be just as guilty of not taking risks or not trying new things. Regardless of age, curiosity is a motivational state that can emerge, change focus, or end abruptly depending on the circumstances. Much of the time, people may not try to learn more about themselves and how others view them until circumstances force them into it. Stephen is a perfect example of this. Recently, Stephen lost the job he had held for eighteen years. The day he was fired, his boss inadvertently revealed that several of Stephen's colleagues found him to be rigid and unapproachable. Stephen's wife has given him this feedback for years, but when he heard his boss say it on the day he lost his job, the comment stuck with him. When he met with his outplacement consultant, Stephen confided in her that he was embarrassed to have been viewed as inflexible by his peers. There were probably many signs that people at

Stephen's company felt this way about him, but sadly, he wasn't motivated to pay attention to this feedback until it was too late to salvage the situation.

Other people become more curious and introspective as they age. They do a kind of life review assessment, and become motivated to make changes in those attitudes and behaviors that did not work well for them in the past. The key of curiosity is naturally a huge driver in this process. Reading about each of the Eleven Keys will help you discover your areas of strength and the areas you need to work on. Make a list of five or six people you trust and whose opinions you respect. Write down each person's name and relationship to you here.

_____

_____

_____

_____

_____

_____

Next, think of several specific questions you can ask each person on your list. Ask them to answer honestly to help you learn more about yourself. Here are some examples.

- What is one thing I can do more of to enhance our relationship?
- Can you name three qualities or traits I have that you wouldn't change?
- If you could change one thing about me, what would it be and why?
- Do I have a strength that you think I could use in a different, more effective way?

- If you could give me one piece of advice to help me succeed at work, what would it be?

Receiving candid answers to these or similar questions is a great way to help you learn more about yourself and become more thoughtful about how you react and behave at work.

Write Your Own Eulogy

This exercise is typically used with people who are going through a transition of some kind and need to become more knowledgeable about themselves in order to make the transition successful. Find a quiet place to sit down and write two paragraphs that someone who knows you would read at your funeral or memorial service. Be as candid as possible and focus on the truth.

If during your search for satisfying work, you feel stymied or frustrated, review the Eleven Keys to Success. If you focus on them, you will remain grounded and secure in the knowledge that you can make the changes you need to find satisfying work!

CHAPTER 12

Job Search–the Nuts and Bolts

Your Job Search

Jason Alba founded JibberJobber when he was laid off and realized there was nothing available to keep the many moving parts of a job search organized. When asked what advice he would give to job seekers who feel overwhelmed by all the things they need to do to be effective in their search, he replied: "Find principle-based strategies for your job search and stick with them. People are realizing that networking and branding are more important than their educational credentials. The necessity of categorizing, tracking, and maintaining your relationships and understanding how others perceive you and what you can do to help perpetuate this is crucial."

At times during your search you may feel overwhelmed, frustrated, intimidated, uncomfortable, insecure, rejected, and/or depressed. Experiencing any of these emotions is completely normal. Some people you encounter will be arrogant or insensitive or behave unprofessionally. This, too, is normal. On the positive side, there will be times when you are likely to feel euphoric, hopeful, excited, and self-confident. In fact, your job search process may amplify such positive emotions to the point where you'll wish that you could "bottle" them. Many of the people whom you will talk to or meet with will be kind, professional, complimentary, and optimistic about your chances of landing the job or work situation of your dreams. You should expect some or many of these behaviors and reactions "to come with the territory" as you continue the search for work that you love.

Now that you know where you are and where you want to be in your career, here are some tools that you can use while looking for a job. Regardless of the condition of the job market or how great an influence technology may have on the workplace, certain fundamental truths about the process of looking for a job will always remain the same.

Relationships Are Essential to Changing Jobs

The harder you work at nurturing your existing relationships, developing new ones, and revitalizing old ones, the easier and more rewarding the job search process will be for you. A relationship is not someone on a list of contacts with whom you have no real connection. A relationship involves interaction between two people in which there is consistent communication. The individuals involved are familiar with each other's work and perhaps even their life situation. Trust exists, and both people are interested in helping the other. It is a bonus when the two people in the relationship share common interests or goals and really like each other. Since relationships require a great deal of hard work, many people just aren't willing to do what is necessary to create and cultivate them. Whether or not you are conducting a job search, part of your work should always be creating new relationships and nurturing the ones you have.

What if you have let go of many of your relationships because you've buried yourself in your work? Contrary to what many people think, it is easier and makes more sense to rekindle the relationships you've let go than to try to develop new ones. The person you have had a relationship with in the past already knows you, so trust and rapport can be reignited more easily. If you haven't talked with someone in a while, it is always interesting to hear about what's changed in that person's life and work situation. She may have been wondering about you and feeling uncomfortable because she, too, hasn't done much lately to foster your relationship, and now you've done the hard part by getting in touch with her first. People inherently like to be helpful to others and are more inclined to do so with someone they already know.

New relationships are also very important in a successful job search. Ask your existing friends and acquaintances for referrals to people they know with whom you can talk. Since people tend to respond to someone they don't know if the introduction is made through someone they do, make sure to acknowledge the person whom you have in common. When beginning new relationships it is important to communicate that although you obviously are seeking their assistance, you are also approaching them to begin a mutually fulfilling relationship. This means that well after you are settled in your new job or career, you should continue to nurture these new relationships.

Social media can help you reconnect with people from your past and develop new relationships; however, relationships are strongest when they involve a variety of different types of interaction—from texting and e-mailing to grabbing a coffee together or attending a group networking meeting.

You Must Know Yourself

The clearer you are about your preferences, likes and dislikes, strengths and weaknesses—the essence of who you are—the more straightforward your job search process will be. By now you have gone over your self-assessments several times and have a clear sense of who you are and what you want. If you don't, go back to the chapters that describe your situation and review your self-assessments.

When you are ready to launch your job search, it is essential that you are able to tell other people, both orally and in writing, who you are, how this translates to what you are looking for, and how you can contribute and make a difference in the work you are pursuing. In the heat of a job search, people often have great difficulty articulating their interests or the ways they made improvements in previous jobs. Instead, the nervous interviewee tends to talk only about his or her present or past job tasks, responsibilities, and skills. This tendency, coupled with the likelihood that the person doing the interviewing may not be a skilled interviewer, can be a recipe for an unsuccessful job interview.

Interviews are not the only situation where it is important to articulate who you are and what you are looking for. Informational meetings, casual conversations, and introductions in meetings with people who don't know you are all opportunities to succinctly demonstrate who you are and what you have to offer.

How can you prepare to talk about yourself in a meaningful way for interviews or other opportunities?

1. Think about an accomplishment you achieved in a previous job by answering these questions using Fred's following situation as an example.

   What was an obstacle, challenge, or situation that needed to be changed or improved in your job?

   _____

   _____

   _____

   _____

Fred, a human resources manager, noticed that employee turnover on the hourly levels was very high.

What did you do to change or improve it?

_____

_____

_____

_____

Fred began surveying hourly workers about their working conditions and the reasons they were dissatisfied. He then asked them for suggestions about ways to make their work more satisfactory. Using this information, Fred created a program just for hourly workers that encompassed small bonuses for meeting goals, flextime, and an allowance for technical education, and he turned an unused conference room into an employee lounge.

What was the result of the changes you made? (Use quantifiable measurements if you can, like percentages and numbers.)

_____

_____

_____

_____

Fred began tracking the hourly employee turnover rate, which went from 80 percent before he started the program to 55 percent six months after the program was in place.

2. Write down your accomplishment in one succinct sentence.

Fred can say, "I reduced hourly employee turnover from eighty percent to fifty-five percent by implementing a special program that motivated and rewarded hourly workers."

3. Identify three accomplishments for each job you've held, including your current position, and write them down.

What was an obstacle, challenge, or situation that needed to be changed or improved in your job?

What did you do to change or improve it? (Use quantifiable measurements if you can, like percentages and numbers.)

What was the result of the changes you made?

_____

_____

_____

_____

Have a Focused and Flexible Plan with Realistic, Achievable Goals

Having a written, focused, and flexible plan that includes specific action steps for achieving your goals and objectives will help ensure that you will reach your destination. A plan will also help you avoid wasting time doing things that are counterproductive.

It is ironic that when we embark on something as meaningful as looking for a job or changing careers, we rarely put a large amount of effort into planning and goal setting. Although this may be because we lack the motivation or the skills to plan, it is usually because of a psychological mind-set that accompanies our approach to a job search. Too often we become overwhelmed by the process, and yet a plan can and should be simple, specific, and flexible, with goals that are realistic, quantifiable, and small. Here is an example: Sam said he wanted a senior marketing position within the consumer products industry, specifically in food and beverages. He wanted to secure this new career within six months and was determined to find it by actively networking with everyone he had ever met. He set the realistic goal for himself of talking with two people every week about his plan. Sam's criterion for identifying people was anyone who he felt was approachable, liked him, knew a lot of other people, or actually worked in consumer products. Using this criterion, he was able to create a long list of people. Within three months he landed a marketing executive position in New Jersey, working for an old college friend.

You should always write down your plan. Here is a sample:

My Job Search   Week of _____

These are my three primary goals:

1. Finish my résumé and show it to three people for feedback.

   Did I do this?   *Yes*   *No*
   Notes:

   _____

   _____

   _____

2. Make a list of fifteen people to contact on LinkedIn, via e-mail, or on the phone.

   Did I do this?   *Yes*   *No*
   Notes:

   _____

   _____

   _____

3. Call five people on this list with the goal of setting up a face-to-face meeting with each one.

   Did I do this?   *Yes*   *No*
   Notes:

   _____

Save your plans each week, keeping them in one place so that you can refer to them if you need to.

You Must Make Decisions and Take Action

A plan is essential, but if you fail to make decisions or to act on the decisions you do make, your job search will be futile. Decisions drive action. Without action—making phone calls, following up those calls, setting up meetings, and scheduling interviews—it is impossible to find a new job or make the changes you'd like to make in your work. The inability to make decisions can stem from many things, including insecurity, lack of passion, and fear—fear of success, fear of failure, and fear of change or the unknown. The irony is that taking action and experiencing success is the best possible remedy for overcoming fear and vanquishing insecurity. As for not having passion, this means that either you are pursuing something you think you should do or someone else wants for you, or you simply don't have enough information. We humans just don't make decisions if we aren't motivated to do so. The first step to making decisions is learning what your motivation is.

Harold, a vice president of training, hired a career coach because he had no passion for his career and at age forty was feeling inordinately dissatisfied and unhappy. In his first meeting with his coach, Harold told her that his biggest problem, in his view, was that he was incapable of making decisions. He had changed careers twice in the past but did so easily because people he knew brought him into those jobs at a time in his life when he was younger and more flexible. Since then he had pursued careers in law, advertising, and the nonprofit sector. In each instance he had been made an offer or was set to embark on the next step when he became paralyzed about making a decision that would move him into a new career.

Harold began to create a plan every week that enabled him to make small decisions about researching industries, networking with people, answering Internet ads, and finding opportunities. He experienced a lot of highs and lows during his search, but a year and a half later he did find a job with a public relations firm. He credits his success to getting into the habit of asking himself, "What's the next decision I need to make about my job search?" until making decisions became habitual for him and no longer an obstacle.

The Most Important Elements of a Job Search

Your Résumé

The first thing that many people think about when deciding to embark on a job search is writing a résumé. Most companies still rely on résumés to learn about a candidate's work history and use it as a tool when interviewing. Another reason for knowing who you are, what you want, and what you have to offer is that you can put this information on your résumé. Although a résumé serves as documentation of your career history, it has three even more important purposes:

1. Writing a good résumé requires you to spend quality time thinking about who you are and the impact you've made in the past. Once you have done this, it will be much easier for you to handle face-to-face discussions with a networking contact or interviewer.

2. You can creatively describe your experiences and accomplishments in a way that can effectively match the prospective employer's needs.

3. The opportunity to express your unique personality traits and skills on paper can help you distinguish yourself from other candidates.

Writing a résumé that tells a compelling story to a human reader and can also be easily scanned by applicant tracking system software is extremely important. There is usually no need to create multiple versions of your résumé.

Elements That Need to Be on a Résumé

Profile or summary: This is a paragraph or list of bulleted statements that captures your experience and key competencies or strengths, and that emphasizes your knowledge, skills, and qualifications for the job you are seeking. This is the place to add a few characteristics or qualities that personalize your résumé and make you memorable.

Keywords section: There are hundreds of thousands of jobs listed online on job boards and company Web sites, and you'll need to create a résumé with corresponding keywords. These keywords are generally technical in nature and usually placed at the beginning of your résumé as part of your summary or in a separate section. For example, keywords might be "Raisers Edge," "nonprofit," "supply chain management," "advocacy," and "capital campaign planning."

Banner heading: The old résumé "objective" has made a comeback. This is useful for succinctly explaining what type of job you are looking for, and as another visible place to list keywords.

Chronological organization: List all the jobs you've had in your career in the order you held them. Sometimes people will create a functional/chronological version with the goal of covering up gaps in employment. This version is not as acceptable to potential employers, particularly recruiters or human resource professionals.

Functional focus: Descriptions of the jobs in your career history should be customized to align with the job you are applying for.

Achievements: Verb-heavy with a focus on action. Examples of action verbs are *succeeded, originated, devised, created,* and *managed.* There are several formulas used to write an achievement (also called an accomplishment). The easiest is C-A-R: What was the *challenge* that needed solving; what *action* did you take to solve it; what was the *result* you reached that made a positive difference (quantified numerically if possible).

Formatting: Should be as simple and plain as possible without unusual fonts or graphic elements. Italics, underlining, tables, and certain bullets can confuse scanning software. The exception is for creative professionals, who usually create several formats, one traditional and the second creatively designed with hyperlinks and infographics—graphic visual representations of data that simplify information in a visually engaging way, such as graphs, charts, and feature sections.

Résumé length and content: One page for a recent college graduate and two pages for anyone else. Typically a résumé captures only the past ten to fifteen years; the content should be short and snappy.

Volunteer or community service: This is great to add because it shows the causes with which you spend time outside of work. It is important to list your achievements in this section as well, even if you were not paid.

Your résumé represents you and is often what people use to assess you even before you meet. Because of this, you should write the best résumé possible. On the other hand, spending more time writing your résumé than planning your job search strategy will not be the best use of your time.

Targeting Potential Employers

As a career coach, one of the first recommendations I make to clients once they have finished the packaging elements of their job search, such as updating their résumé and online profiles, is to create a target list of companies and their key employees to both follow and network with. There are several reasons this is an effective strategy for job seekers. By identifying companies that may potentially be a good fit for you, you are taking a more proactive approach rather than waiting for jobs to open up with companies that you know nothing about or may not even be interested in working for.

So many jobs are not "advertised" at all, and for this reason alone, it is a good idea to be knowledgeable about companies. More and more companies are creating openings as they meet talented people whom they think can produce results. You can follow companies on LinkedIn and research them on Glassdoor.com, a Web site where employees and former employees anonymously post reviews of companies and their management. Additionally, many employers offer incentives to their employees for referring talented professionals; therefore, staying up-to-date with friends, neighbors, and former colleagues about their employers is a good idea.

Networking

Networking will always be an important part of the job search process, so you should become comfortable with it. Statistically, 80 percent or more of jobs are found by networking. Learning to network is analogous to learning how to ride a bicycle. When you were little, it seemed so impossible to learn to ride a two-wheeler. But once you learned how, it was exhilarating at first and then became second nature. Now you can't imagine not being able to remember how to ride a bike. If you've gone a while without riding one, you will feel a bit wobbly at first, but then you will hit your familiar stride.

Fear of the unknown is perfectly normal. Being fearful of unpleasant experiences is normal, too. If you are fearful of networking, the best way to handle your anxiety is to think of the worst possible scenario. Ask yourself, "What's the worst that could happen?" Chances are your fear will be harder to deal with than the actual negative or unpleasant outcome that might result from your taking a risk. If you are fearful of being rejected, remind yourself that it is unlikely people will reject you as a person in a networking situation. They may not take the time to talk with or meet you because they either don't know how to help you or don't see the value in it. Since there are so many people who do engage in networking, it makes sense just to move on if you are getting either a negative response or no response from a particular individual.

Here are some ways to begin the networking process:

1. Make a list of everyone you know and divide them into categories such as professional services, neighbors, former business colleagues, friends, and college alumni. You will be continually surprised by the people who will help you during your networking process, like your dentist or neighbor three doors down.

2. It is ideal if you purchase contact management software such as Act!, or use JibberJobber.com, or even just Outlook to keep your network organized. The idea is to keep all the names and contact information in one place, as well as to track your conversations, meetings, and follow-up.

3. Before you e-mail or call anyone on your list, write a brief script stating what it is you're looking for. Be specific and succinct. Your script will have an introduction, something like "I can't believe it's been two years since we've talked. How are you doing?" Then describe what you're doing in one or two sentences: "I'm calling you because I've decided to make a career change, and I had heard that you did the same thing about a year ago." The last part of the script discusses a next step: "I'd be so appreciative if we could spend twenty minutes together so that you can share your experience with me. When would this be convenient for you?" Be sure to mention that you would like to help them in any way that makes sense as well so it doesn't feel like a one-way conversation.

4. Go to the networking meeting prepared with a résumé (if appropriate) and a business card. (Even if you are unemployed, have

simple business cards printed with your name and contact information.) You should also know what two or three pieces of information you are looking for. Are you looking for feedback on your résumé or the names of people at a specific company? If you don't do this, the information you gather may not be useful to you.

5. Always ask the person if there is anything you can do to help him or her. The person could be looking for a new babysitter or is trying to buy a new car, and you may be able to offer help as well.

6. Your networking style is crucial. The impression you make really matters. Be sure that you look and sound professional and confident. Don't ramble on and on about yourself.

7. Any gathering of people presents an opportunity for you to network. Baseball games, association meetings, your neighborhood block party, and the grocery store are all full of people who are familiar with what's going on in the business world and know other people.

8. Always send a thank-you note or e-mail to the person immediately after your meeting. Say that you plan to stay in touch periodically. You should initiate follow-up, particularly if the person has offered to send you someone's name or other information.

9. Online social networking is a significant element of networking; however, it will never replace traditional face-to-face networking. It is a good idea to update your profile regularly on the social networking Web sites of your choice, such as LinkedIn, as well as to reach out to your online connections, posting and answering questions and writing and requesting recommendations. A word of caution: The majority of employers and headhunters will Google you or go directly to your online networking profiles. If you or your friends have posted inappropriate photos or comments on your Facebook or Google+ profiles, this can mar your professional reputation and possibly damage your chances of getting an interview.

Networking is a life skill, not just something you do when you are changing jobs. The more you practice it, the more useful it will become to you, not only during your time of transition but even when you are happily working.

Responding to Online Postings

While job boards are very useful job search tools, they are no longer the primary way to get a job and haven't been for quite a while. Although most companies list job openings on their Web sites, they are becoming much more creative and resourceful in their approaches to recruiting new employees—placing ads on buses and subways or on Craigslist, for example. Proactively sourcing potential candidates on social media (LinkedIn, Facebook, Twitter, etc.) has become a primary method for filling job openings for many companies. Many organizations offer financially rewarding referral programs for existing employees with links on their company Web sites that list descriptions of current job openings.

By all means, answer postings if you'd like, keeping in mind that this conventional method is not always the most warm, interactive, or multidimensional way to communicate with a potential employer. It can be beneficial to network with an employee of the company even though you have applied for a job opening online.

Contingency and Search Firms

Contingency firms are used by companies to find candidates in a specific salary range—usually under $100,000. They don't normally sign a contract with the company for whom they are recruiting candidates and are paid a fee only when a candidate is hired. Search (or retainer) firms are used by companies for filling senior-level positions, typically those that pay $100,000 or more. Search firms sign an agreement and receive their fee in installments even if they never find a candidate who is hired by the company.

Both types of firms have one client: the company that hires them. Most of the time if you are a job candidate who has been contacted by a search or contingency firm, you will feel as if the recruiter or search professional does not have your best interests at heart. It will seem as if they pay attention to you only when they think you might be a fit for a specific opening. And you will be absolutely right! The sooner you realize and accept this fact, the less frustrated you will be when dealing with contingency and search firms.

Go ahead and work with search or contingency firms, but do not rely solely on them to find your next job for you. In most cases they will only be able to place you if you are looking for exactly the same type of position in the industry you work in now. *Rarely is a search firm paid a fee for placing a candidate who is making a career change.* Still, it's smart to develop long-standing relationships with search or contingency professionals even if they can't place you. Connect with them on LinkedIn, refer candidates to them, and always return their calls when they leave a message asking whom you might know for a search they are working on. A search or contingency professional is a good person to develop a networking relationship with over time. Just remember that they are salespeople whose compensation is contingent upon placing individuals with specific skills in specific jobs.

Interviewing

It is highly unusual to find a new job without going on a face-to-face interview, and these days, it is also common to meet and talk to a large number of people in an organization during the hiring process. In fact, job seekers are enduring more extensive interviewing processes, which might involve being asked to deliver a presentation, undertake trial projects and assignments, or solve a business case—sometimes even without preparation—with several people observing. If you are not capable of making an impressive presentation to the people with whom you are interviewing, you will not receive a job offer.

Companies are much more cautious about seeing job candidates in person for first, second, or sometimes even third interviews. Phone interviews are still the most popular method used to screen candidates, with video screening using Skype, Google Hangouts, join.me, and FaceTime increasing in popularity. It is crucial that you prepare just as thoroughly for these types of interviews as you would for an in-person interview.

"Performing" well in interviews means several things: Your physical image must be appealing to the interviewer; your verbal presentation must be interesting and focused on what you can bring to and do for the interviewer and his or her company; and you must demonstrate that you will fit well in the organization. Companies also are relying on personality testing and other assessments to determine fit.

Interviewing, while stressful for many people, is a learned skill. Being prepared to talk about yourself and your past accomplishments succinctly and in a compelling manner is very important. If you've gone through some assessment and written a quality résumé, then you already are familiar with all this information. Since you probably don't go on interviews every day, it is difficult to practice, but before going on a significant interview, ask friends, family, or a career coach to role-play with you. Oddly enough, most people don't do this.

It seems obvious to talk about the importance of answering questions effectively; however, even if you prepare your answers prior to your interview, there are a handful of questions that typically seem to stump interviewees. Here are some of these questions.

- Tell me about yourself.
- What are your weaknesses or areas for development?
- Why do you want to work here?
- Tell me about a time when you failed at something.
- Why did you leave your last job?
- Why is there a gap on your résumé?
- What kind of compensation are you looking for?
- Why should we hire you?

Additionally, behavioral interviewing is a very common interviewing technique that companies use. The questions are focused on how you have acted in specific job situations, with the logic being that the ways you behaved in the past will provide a strong indication of how your behavior will repeat in similar situations.

So, in addition to being asked how you would behave under certain conditions (how would you respond to . . .; how would you feel about . . .; how would you adjust when . . .), you may be asked how you did behave (give me an example of when you had to . . .).

Bottom line, you are there to sell both your technical skills and experience and your personal behavioral traits.

While preparing to answer questions yourself, you may also want to prepare a list of questions for the interviewer and anyone else you meet at the company. You can write down their answers, compare them later, and use the information to write customized thank-you notes. Here are some questions you might want to ask.

- What do you think an average day in this position would be like?
- What would be your expectations of me in my first three months? Six months? A year?
- What are the biggest problems or challenges you are facing in this department or division?
- What reporting relationships would I have in this job?
- What kinds of people succeed here?
- What were the strengths of the person who was in this job previously?
- How would you describe the corporate culture here?

Remember that many people aren't necessarily very skilled at interviewing candidates. It is therefore your responsibility as the interviewee to keep the conversation on track so that (1) you can communicate everything you need to the interviewer before the interview ends, and (2) you will get the information you need in order to move forward in the process.

Branding

A significant aspect of the job search is the concept of branding yourself. While large companies have had marketing departments who have done this for years, it is recommended that those of you who are reinventing yourselves or simply looking for another job similar to one you've had should do the same thing.

The Career Thought Leaders Consortium published career management trends in a 2015 report in which they shared the following findings about personal branding:

- Personal branding and reputation management are growing in importance.
- Personal branding will soon be taught in high school and college in order to help younger people identify their skills, professional interests, and unique characteristics to better equip them for making job and career choices.
- YouTube provides an excellent, far-reaching platform for ongoing personal branding.
- Personal stories help get personal branding messages out there.
- LinkedIn is a place to brand yourself as a candidate to attract potential employers.
- People with disabilities, those with long gaps in employment, and former military personnel, etc., struggle with branding because their situations are not typical.

Implementing your brand can be accomplished in many ways, including the following:

- Write a blog.
- Respond to others' blog posts.
- Write and publish articles in professional and trade publications and on Web sites.
- Post and answer questions and post updates on LinkedIn.

- Create your own personal Web site. Even if you don't design it right now, go to GoDaddy.com or Homestead.com and purchase and register a domain name.
- Have someone help you to design a Web folio. This is an expanded document that focuses on your achievements as they relate to leadership and professional competencies throughout your career and is accessible online. Your résumé can be embedded in it as well.
- Conduct polls on LinkedIn or other social networking sites.
- Present at professional conferences or to nonprofit groups.
- Tweet meaningful content on Twitter.

Follow-up

Writing thank-you notes is a very important method of follow-up for both networking meetings and actual interviews. Whether your thanks are handwritten or in an e-mail isn't really the issue. Just do it! It adds to the positive impression the interviewer has of you. It also is an additional opportunity to sell yourself and to address any concerns on the interviewer's part that may have come up during the interview. Joanne, the vice president of human resources at an international trading company, observed that, sadly, only 10 percent of the applicants she interviews for nonexempt jobs and 50 percent of the applicants she interviews for exempt or managerial positions send thank-you notes. Marj, a director of human resources at a large utility, stated, "I think thank-you letters are becoming rarer and rarer, regardless of the job levels." This is too bad, since, as she explains, these notes are another tool an applicant has. "They are a good way for a candidate to remind the interviewer of his or her name, reiterate interest in the position, and do a little sales pitch, too."

Everyone has had some experience looking for a job. Regardless of what this has been, there are several false beliefs about looking for a job that perpetually circulate and people seem to accept. This next section addresses the most prevalent myths and the truth about them.

Job Search Myths

Myths that people believe about looking for a job are many and persistent. The most common ones are these:

Myth #1: A résumé should be only one page.

Absolutely not! The normal length of a résumé is two to three pages (at most). It is fine to have addendum pages such as a list of references or published articles. A one-page résumé is only appropriate for a recent college grad.

Myth #2: If you go on an interview through a contingency or search firm, you cannot speak directly to the person(s) at the company who interviewed you after the interview.

The person who interviewed you is either a decision maker or an influencer in the hiring process. Ask him during the interview if he minds if you contact him with any questions you may have later. If he says no, be skeptical about his interest or style. After all, you are the person who was on the interview, not the recruiting professional who set up your interview. He or she is also someone you can nurture as a networking contact even if you aren't hired, so invite him or her to connect with you on LinkedIn.

Myth #3: If eight people at a company interviewed you, you need to send a thank-you note or e-mail only to the person you'd report to if you got the job.

Those other seven people took their valuable time to interview you. Of course you should send each one a thank-you note! Be sure to customize each note based on your specific conversation with each person.

Myth #4: You shouldn't take notes during an interview.

Why not? Nobody has a photographic memory while talking, listening, and processing information. Simply ask the interviewer politely if she minds if you take some notes. Obviously, you should use abbreviations or keywords so that you're not concentrating too hard on taking notes and not focusing enough on the conversation.

Myth #5: There is no point in conducting a job search during the summer or in December because companies aren't hiring then.

This is absolutely ridiculous. In fact, during the summer, businesspeople are more casual and "laid-back" in their attitudes and approaches. They don't tend to be as immersed in stressful projects. What a great time to approach people! In December, companies may be focused on bringing someone on board before the new calendar or fiscal year. People are in a much more celebratory mood during this time of year, and December offers lots of opportunities for networking.

Myth #6: The most qualified candidate has the best shot at getting a job offer.

Obviously, for most positions, a company needs someone with specific skills and experience. It is also true that many companies still lean toward someone who has worked in the same industry. It is more likely that the individual who *fits* into the company culture is the one who will get the offer. This means that as a candidate you are accountable for finding out and understanding what the culture is—the values that shape the company, the way people communicate, and the kinds of people who are respected within the organization. You will not find this kind of information on a Web site or in an annual report. You will find it from talking to people—the company's employees, vendors, and ex-employees.

Myth #7: Only certain components of a job offer are negotiable.

The two best times to negotiate with a company are when they ask you to join them and when they ask you to leave.

Anything can be negotiated if you are very clear about what you need and want, and can state the reasons why. You stand the best chance of getting your needs met if you put yourself in the company's shoes during the negotiation. Not only can compensation be negotiated but also the work itself, the way you will do the work, whom you will report to, and every other aspect of the job.

Myth #8: Human resources or in-house recruiting doesn't influence the hiring decision.

Just because the HR or recruiting professionals don't work in the department in which you'd be hired doesn't mean that the company doesn't listen to their opinions or advice. They are well versed in the corporate culture, the hiring manager's preferences and personality, and the challenges in the department or division. Instead of dismissing HR professionals as unknowledgeable about law, marketing, finance, or whatever your functional area is, appreciate and take advantage of the insight they can provide and the influence they can wield.

Trends and Predictions

There are fundamental elements of the job search that are likely to stay the test of time. You will still need to provide documentation about your work history, meet people in person so they can decide if they should hire you, and, whether it is called social media or something else in the future, develop a digital presence and identity. However, there are also many ways that the workplace and job search have changed and will continue to evolve:

• Thanks to the current educational evolution, people will be able to create their own customized degrees and build a portfolio of certified skills rather than earning a degree, and vocational school education will make a significant comeback.

• More and more people in a job search will hire a professional to help them navigate the process of getting a job. It is extremely difficult from a time standpoint to conduct an effective job search while working, and it can be very isolating while unemployed. Hiring a career coach, résumé and social media profile writer, or branding expert can provide invaluable advice and support, not to mention jump-start the process and shorten the time it takes to find a new job.

• At the same time, job seekers are becoming much more sophisticated about what they need to do to find their next job, given the multiple times many people have been laid off and had to conduct yet another job search. And there is a growing number of people who are dissatisfied in their jobs and choose to quit and dedicate all their time to discovering their next career path.

• More companies will give priority to job seekers who are introduced to them by someone they trust. This is already somewhat true; however, as the more traditional methods of recruiting become less effective and more costly, interviewing and hiring people who are known entities will be given preference.

• The strategy of hiring people as temporary employees and moving them to permanent status will become more prevalent. Whether temporary is defined as an intern, extern, subcontractor, or freelancer, this is a more effective way for companies to try out employees and for individuals to learn about companies. In fact, jobs are becoming more project-based. In the United States, forty-eight of the fifty states have "at-will" employment, meaning that an employee can be dismissed by an employer for any reason (that is, without having to establish "just cause" for termination) and without warning.

• Companies will be more proactive about hiring diverse candidates beyond the traditional definition of diversity—race, religion, nationality, and gender; this means the LGBTQA community, persons with disabilities, and ex-convicts, among others.

Looking for a new job requires many skills and a lot of patience, and the more you network, interview, and negotiate, the easier the process becomes. Above all, trust your instincts during your job search. As with any relationship, you may have to make compromises. However, there is absolutely no reason that you shouldn't be able to find the right job—a job that fits your personality and fulfills your needs.

Afterword

Gallup Poll's survey in late 2013 showed that worker satisfaction was continuing to spiral downward from previous years, with an alarming 70 percent of Americans feeling negative about their jobs and going as far as saying that they either hated their jobs or were completely disengaged.

These statistics point to a pervasive, consistent dissatisfaction in the workplace today. On the other hand, it is now both accepted and expected that if you are unhappy, bored, or unfulfilled in your work, you *can* and *should* change what you are doing. In a CareerBuilder survey of 3,008 workers nationwide in late 2014, one in five said that they plan to change jobs in the next year. The top reasons they would like new jobs? No advancement opportunities, dissatisfaction with work-life balance, feeling underemployed, experiencing high levels of stress, a poor opinion of their boss's performance, feeling as if they were overlooked for a promotion, and no pay increase.

Work is no longer just about completing tasks to make money for a company and its shareholders. Instead, it is about creating and maintaining a more equitable relationship between employee and employer or business owner and client. It is also about you as an individual needing and wanting choices, meaning, rewards, motivation, and success in your work. The path is different for each of us. If you are feeling dissatisfied or disillusioned with your current job, then your mission is not only to admit that you are dissatisfied but to also commit to creating a vision for the kind of work that will bring you satisfaction and to design a plan for implementing your vision. You can begin the journey of finding gratifying work right now!

There are thousands upon thousands of people who have successfully changed their work to reflect their needs and preferences. Here are a few stories of people who have done so and are happy.

Rita is a self-employed media consultant. At forty-six she has taken what she's learned in the six careers she's already had (recruiting, the restaurant business, social services counseling, real estate sales, corporate relocation, and advertising sales) and created interesting new work for herself. "I've always wanted to do work that matters to me. I need to be passionate about what I do, and I want to excel at it. Recently, I stepped off the cliff of the more secure corporate environment and have been successful in establishing myself as an independent consultant—*and* I have enough work to be financially secure."

Greg, fifty-two, was a lawyer for twenty years. "I had to give in to the creative parts of me that I had not been pursuing during that career," he says. So he decided to stop practicing law and become a photographer. He now reports: "My job gives me the opportunity to make things with my hands, which is a kind of creativity that is most important to me."

At thirty-six, Jon was let go during a downsizing from his job as a corporate human resources executive. He intentionally took more than a year off from working to "figure out what I wanted to do." Why? While he was successful in his job, he did not find it fulfilling. "I thought I was sophisticated when I started my introspective journey and found it more difficult than I had expected. There's no language and no definite path to searching for the right work. I do feel that there is a path that is different for everyone." While Jon knows he needs to find challenging and engaging work, at the same time he wants to live a more holistic life, something he believes is difficult to do while one is caught up in the corporate whirlwind.

During his hiatus, Jon went through an extensive rediscovery process using the Crystal-Barkley method (*The Crystal-Barkley Guide to Taking Charge of Your Career* by Nella Barkley and Eric Sandburg), which included writing a thirty-page story of his life. What did he decide to do? He thinks he'll end up in human resources again, but with an employer who believes strongly in human capital and isn't simply focused on making a profit. Now that he has refreshed his understanding of himself and what is important to him, Jon feels better equipped to find fulfillment—as opposed to just "success"— in his work.

While it is important to experience tangible success in your work—that is, achieving the business goals that you and your employer have set—once you have done this, the meaning can fade quickly. Teri, thirty-five, sells a music service. She has ranked as the number one salesperson in her company for six years. Teri is Bored and has Plateaued. "Who cares if I make the top of the list again?" she says. "It just does not mean anything to me anymore." Teri is planning a start-up venture, manufacturing and selling acrylic frames for parents' ultrasound pictures of their babies in utero. "This is a project from my heart, so I love it," says Teri. "It fuels my creative side. This will be a huge challenge—I cannot wait."

Miguel practiced law his entire career. At sixty he bought a wine store franchise, opening a brand-new location for the franchisor. In his first six months Miguel's sales ranked in the top percentage of all the company's franchises in the United States. More important, Miguel is "extremely satisfied and gratified to be working for myself and deciding on my own destiny and future." Miguel had been in the Yearning to Be on Your Own situation for a long time because "I was tired and fed up working for incompetent managers who were where they were because of who they knew and not what they knew. I just wanted to be the 'captain of my own ship.'"

Jack retired at sixty-three from a thirty-year career in the chemical industry. At sixty-nine he works full-time as a senior consultant for a research company that supports his former industry. He holds three significant leadership roles for volunteer organizations as well. When Jack isn't working sixty hours a week, he flies a plane, sails, kayaks, and collects cameras. When Jack was asked how long he thought he'd keep working, he replied, "Probably another ten years."

In her book *What Do You Want to Do When You Grow Up?*

psychologist Dorothy Cantor makes an important point that "previously defined visions can fade in importance over time. Life keeps happening, and transitions are part of it." The point of this book is to help you realize that being satisfied, happy, fulfilled, or exhilarated with your work is up to you and you alone.

Six years ago, Jody read the second edition of this book and says that it changed her life. She read it when she was unhappy in her job and was ready to make the next move, but, she said, "I didn't know enough about myself to know where to go." A graphic artist at the time, Jody says she "thought I wanted to be my own boss and start a creative freelance company. By the end of the book, I realized that being creative was just a small part of a much larger picture. I am now in the process of getting my doctorate in a field I discovered in the book (e-learning)! I found my passion and made it my job—talk about awesome!" Jody is happily employed as a digital instructional designer in organization development for a large consumer products company.

It is time to make yourself happy in your work. Start your journey today. As Jon, the human resources executive, said earlier, it's not necessarily easy to find your path toward finding satisfying work. This is why more people choose *not* to do anything about alleviating their unhappiness or dissatisfaction. Don't let yourself be one of them. Instead, close your eyes and allow yourself to imagine what it would feel like to be happy and excited and fulfilled in your work. Finding work that is satisfying, gratifying, and fulfilling will change your life!

Resources

Chapter 1: Why Do You Want or Need to Change Your Work?

Books

The Balance Myth: Rethinking Work-Life Success by Teresa A. Taylor. Greenleaf Book Group Press, 2013. Advice on achieving a successful work-life balance in today's demanding world. The author tells us her story and insights of how she ascended through the ranks to become COO of a Fortune 200 company while raising two boys with her working husband. A great read for anyone who feels torn between their home and professional lives.

Generations at Work: Managing the Clash of Boomers, Gen Xers, and Gen Yers in the Workplace by Ron Zemke, Claire Raines, and Bob Filipczak. AMACOM, 2013. Offers practical guidelines for managing the differences in the multigenerational workplace. Includes in-depth interviews with members of each generation; best practices from companies bridging the generation gap; specific tips for each generation on how to handle the others; and a field guide for mentoring Generation Y.

Chapter 2: What Is Your Work Situation?

Books

Be a Free Range Human: Escape the 9 to 5, Create a Life You Love and Still Pay the Bills by Marianne Cantwell. Kogan Page, 2013. A refreshing book that challenges conventional approaches to leaving a corporate job and becoming self-employed while creating a lifestyle that fits your needs.

The Encore Career Handbook: How to Make a Living and a Difference in the Second Half of Life by Marci Alboher. Workman Publishing Company, 2013. This is a comprehensive guide for creating a road map when deciding on and pursuing a new career that combines doing good and fulfilling your practical needs. Alboher is a leading career-change expert.

The Escape Manifesto: Quit Your Corporate Job—Do Something Different! audiobook by Escape the City and narrated by Glen McCready. Audible, 2013. Inspirational call to action to leave your corporate job and find fulfillment by doing something different workwise.

How to Win Your First Great Job: A 30-minute no-nonsense guide to jump-starting your professional career after college by Mike W. Mathies. Mike Mathies, 2015. Easy to read with easy to follow step-by-step instructions that will help you find the role that will launch your professional career.

A Useful Web Site

National Career Development Association: www.ncda.org. First established in 1913, the NCDA is the "first, longest running and preeminent career development association in the world." Check out their resources page, which has a huge list of resources, services, and tools to assist you in exploring careers, planning for the future, searching for employment, and finding additional training to pursue your dream.

Chapter 3: Values, Attitudes, and Change Resilience and Chapter 4: Personality Preferences, Interests, and Favorite Skills

Books

Act Like a Leader, Think Like a Leader by Herminia Ibarra. Harvard Business Review Press, 2015. Written by a renowned professor at INSEAD, a leading international business school, this book has self-assessments and practical advice to help clarify your leadership challenges and devise a plan to become a better leader and move your career to the next level.

The Art of Work: A Proven Path to Discovering What You Were Meant to Do by Jeff Goins. Nelson Books, 2015. With personal stories and case studies, along with research as to the essence of motivation and talent, Jeff shows readers how to find their vocation and what they can expect along the path.

The Bliss List: Discover What Truly Makes You Happy—Then Land Your Dream Job by J. P. Hansen. Reader's Digest, 2010. This award-winning book is an insightful and inspirational guide written in a helpful coaching style.

Career Match: Connecting Who You Are with What You'll Love to Do by Shoya Zichy with Ann Bidou. AMACOM, 2007. This older yet still relevant book is entertaining and witty, using a work-style assessment technique called Color Q, which is basically a twist on personality type.

Do What You Are: Discover the Perfect Career for You Through the Secrets of Personality Type by Paul D. Tieger, Barbara Barron, and Kelly Tieger. Little, Brown, 2014, fifth edition. Based on the Myers-Briggs Type Indicator, this book introduces personality types and aligns them with suggested careers. Many occupations are listed that are popular with specific personality types, including careers in biotech, new media, e-commerce, and telecommunications.

Paid to Be You: A Guide to Getting Unstuck, Finding Your Passion, and Launching a New Career by Adam Rico. Broadstone Publishing,

2014. Helps to identify the different components that are needed to finding meaningful and fulfilling work by examining your personality traits, skills, strengths, passions, and dreams to find work that's aligned with who you truly are.

Some Useful Web Sites

CareerBuilder Advice and Resources: http://Advice.CareerBuilder .com. One of the best-known career and job search sites also offers a very comprehensive resource page in which you can search for topics like networking, personal branding, and self-assessment, among many others. Furthermore, you can filter your results by industry or job phase. A great resource for everyone who is looking to start or further his or her career.

CareerPerfect.com. A comprehensive career-planning site with online career-planning tools and tests; advice for and samples of résumés, e-résumés, and cover letters; job search advice and resources; interview advice and tools; and articles on such topics as employment trends and coping with unemployment.

CareerPlanner.com. This site provides information on the career-planning process, a reading list in career planning, and some career-planning tests (some cost a fee to take).

Careers by Design: www.Careers-by-Design.com. This site offers affordable, statistically reliable, and valid assessments (Strong Interest Inventory, MBTI, FIRO-B, 16PF) for individual career planning, determining personality type, and corporate team development.

The MAPP Career Assessment: www.Assessment.com. Designed for students, graduates and working adults, this site caters to all: the unemployed, underemployed, and those just looking for a better job. Provides a fifteen-minute career-aptitude test that will provide you with a list of jobs that are just right for you and get you started in a career that you love.

Chapter 5: Where's the Meaning?

Books

The Artist's Way: A Spiritual Path to Higher Creativity by Julia Cameron. Jeremy P. Tarcher/Putnam, 2002. This classic unfolds a twelve-week program for recovering creativity using journaling as a method for doing so. It was written for artists and people in creative occupations, but it is a useful guide for nonartists as well.

Careers in Renewable Energy: Your World. Your Future by Gregory McNamee. PixyJack Press, Inc., 2014, updated second edition. This book is ideal for students, career changers, and job seekers who are passionate about the greening of the world. Details a variety of career sectors and job areas in which you can make a difference.

Compassionate Careers: Making a Living by Making a Difference by Jeffrey W. Pryor and Alexandra Mitchell. Career Press, 2015. Stories that capture the spirit, intelligence, imagination, and heart of people who have meaningful jobs in cause-focused organizations. A guide to finding purpose-driven work for those who aren't content sitting on the sidelines.

The $100 Startup: Reinvent the Way You Make a Living, Do What You Love, and Create a New Future by Chris Guillebeau. Crown Business, 2012. The author, who himself has traveled the globe while never having a "real job," presents case studies of successful businesses that have been started with minimal amounts of money by people who, in nearly every case, had no special skills but were able to monetize their personal passions.

A Path Appears: Transforming Lives, Creating Opportunity by Nicholas D. Kristof and Sheryl WuDunn. Alfred A. Knopf, 2014. So many people who have had for-profit careers are drawn toward a new career involving making a difference for a cause close to their heart. Kristof and WuDunn share their wisdom and passion for the art and science of giving, identifying successful local and global initiatives, while sharing astonishing stories from the front lines of social progress, showing us all how one person can make a difference.

Volunteer Vacations: Short-Term Adventures That Will Benefit You and Others by Bill McMillon, Doug Cutchins, and Anne Geissinger. Chicago Review Press, 2012, eleventh edition. This is a comprehensive guidebook for people who want to travel and find fulfilling and stimulating temporary work.

The Work: My Search for a Life That Matters by Wes Moore. Spiegel & Grau, 2014. The story of how one young man traced a path through the world to find his life's purpose. Moore tells the stories of change makers who've inspired him and what their lives reveal: that our truest work happens when we serve others.

Some Nonprofit Organizations

American Red Cross: www.RedCross.org; 800-733-2767. This organization helps keep people safe every day as well as in emergencies.

America's Promise Alliance: www.AmericasPromise.org; 703-684-4500. The organization, which is led by Colin Powell, focuses on improving the lives of America's youth through mentoring and other support efforts.

Boys & Girls Clubs of America: www.bgca.org; 404-487-5700. An organization whose goal is to enable all young people, especially those who need us most, to reach their full potential as productive, caring, responsible citizens.

Global Volunteers: www.GlobalVolunteers.org; 800-487-1074. This is a private, international tax-exempt organization in special consultative status with the United Nations.

Habitat for Humanity: www.Habitat.org; 1-800-HABITAT. This organization works in partnership with people in need of building and renovating decent, affordable housing.

National Alliance on Mental Illness (NAMI): www.nami.org; 703-524-7600. Recognized as one of the most formidable grassroots mental-health advocacy organizations in the country, NAMI provides grassroots mental-health education and offers support through programs and advocacy.

Some Useful Web Sites

Bill & Melinda Gates Foundation: www.GatesFoundation.org; 206-709-3100. One of the most prominent philanthropic organizations in the world, this Web site includes information and actionable content on some of the most pressing issues facing the world today.

The Bridgespan Group: www.Bridgespan.org. This Web site helps nonprofits and philanthropies reach their goals and features careers in nonprofit organizations.

Corporation for National & Community Service: www.NationalSer vice.gov. This government-sponsored site promotes volunteering in America and offers tools and information about national and community service to people who want to make a difference through community service and volunteering.

PivotPlanet.com. This innovative Web site pairs you with advisers in more than thirty-five industries such as advertising, agriculture, animals, culinary, design, music, nonprofits, transportation, technology, travel and leisure, and wine. Mentors in hundreds of jobs show you the ropes in their work environments.

VolunteerMatch.org. 415-241-6868. Location-based Web site that helps match you with one of more than ninety thousand nonprofits that need your help all over the world. Includes both local and virtual listings.

Chapter 6: Been There, Done That, but Still Need to Earn

Books

Jim Cramer's Get Rich Carefully by James J. Cramer. Penguin Group, 2001. Cramer draws on his famous knowledge of the stock market to help you navigate the recovering economy and make big money without taking big risks. This book is a fantastic guide to turning savings into real, lasting wealth in a practical and entertaining way.

The Money Class: How to Stand in Your Truth and Create the Future You Deserve by Suze Orman. Spiegel & Grau, 2012. In nine lessons, Orman teaches how to navigate the tumultuous economy. Filled with tools and advice that can lead you from a place of financial uncertainty to financial security.

The Total Money Makeover: Classic Edition: A Proven Plan for Financial Fitness by Dave Ramsey. Nelson Books, 2013. A straightforward approach to completely making over your money habits. Includes plans for paying off all debt, tips on how to recognize the ten most dangerous money myths, and strategies to save a nest egg for emergencies and retirement.

Why Didn't They Teach Me This in School?: 99 Personal Money Management Principles to Live By by Cary Siegel. CreateSpace Independent Publishing, 2015. Includes eight important lessons focusing on ninety-nine principles that will enhance any individual's money management skills. A quick and easily digested read that focuses on the qualities of personal money management.

Chapter 7: Bruised and Gun-shy

Books

Fail Fast, Fail Often: How Losing Can Help You Win by Ryan Babineaux and John Krumboltz. Jeremy P. Tarcher/Penguin, 2013. These authors, who are both psychologists and career counselors, conclude that happy and successful people spend less time planning and more time acting, benefiting from unexpected experiences and opportunities, and showing how to allow enthusiasm to guide you, even when terrified of failure.

HBR Guide to Managing Stress at Work: Renew Your Energy; Lighten the Load; Strike a Better Balance by Harvard Business Review. Harvard Business School Publishing, 2014. This is an anthology of articles originally published individually in HBR that help readers manage their stress and/or their direct reports' stress at work. Divided into four sections, there are practical tips listed on topics such as managing stress in the long term, balancing your job with everything else, and managing stress in the moment.

Keeping Your Head After Losing Your Job: How to Survive Unemployment by Robert Leahy. Behler Publications, 2014. Dr. Leahy has worked with many unemployed people over the years, and his successful techniques draw upon cognitive behavioral therapy and different mindfulness practices to help boost your self-esteem and confidence and develop strength and resilience, and in the process, learn how to live more effectively with a new job.

Reset: How to Get Paid and Love What You Do by Dustin Peterson. Dustin Peterson, 2015. A fresh look at answering the question of what should one do with his or her life, and a straightforward game plan for figuring out how to do your best work while getting paid to be you.

Some Useful Web Sites

The American Institute of Stress: www.stress.org. A nonprofit organization that imparts information on stress reduction, stress in the workplace, effects of stress, and various other stress-related topics.

The Center for Social Epidemiology: www.unhealthywork.org. An educational Web site that provides information about and related to work stress, including occupational causes of ill health, consequences, cures, and resources.

Chapter 8: Bored and Plateaued

Books

Driven to Distraction at Work: How to Focus and Be More Productive by Edward M. Hallowell. HBR Press, 2015. Provides a set of practical and reliable techniques to show how to sustain a productive mental state, identifying the six most common ways people lose the ability to focus at work, and offers advice for training your attention to achieve your highest personal and professional goals.

Love Your Job: The New Rules for Career Happiness by Kerry Hannon. John Wiley & Sons, 2015. A practical book focused specifically on making your current job more rewarding and enjoyable by changing your outlook.

The Pathfinder: How to Choose or Change Your Career for a Lifetime of Satisfaction and Success by Nicholas Lore. Touchstone Books, 2012, updated and revised. This classic bestseller offers invaluable advice and more than one hundred self-tests and diagnostic tools to help you choose an entirely new career or see your current job from a new and more positive perspective. For seasoned professionals and those just entering the workforce, this book provides excellent coaching on crafting a career you will love.

Chapter 9: Yearning to Be on Your Own

Books on Being a Consultant

Case Interview Secrets: A Former McKinsey Interviewer Reveals How to Get Multiple Job Offers in Consulting by Victor Cheng. Innovation Press, 2012. Provides a hands-on, real-world perspective on what it takes to land multiple consulting job offers. For undergraduates, MBAs, PhDs, or experienced candidates, this book details specific performance differences that decide who get management consulting offers from those who don't.

The Consulting Bible: Everything You Need to Know to Create and Expand a Seven-Figure Consulting Practice by Alan Weiss. John Wiley & Sons, 2011. Weiss is the guru of consulting, and *The Consulting Bible* tells you absolutely everything you need to know to create and expand a seven-figure independent or boutique consulting practice.

Flawless Consulting: A Guide to Getting Your Expertise Used by Peter Block. Pfeiffer, 2011, third edition. Time-proven tips from an experienced consultant on how to ask better questions, deal with difficult clients, navigate the virtual workplace, and achieve better implementation. Includes examples and exercises to help you succeed.

I Want to Be a Consultant: How to Get Clear on Your Business Purpose (Consultants' Guide Series 1: Setting Up and Running Your Consultancy Business Profitably and Painlessly) by Cindy Tonkin. Cindy Tonkin, 2014. The first book in a series on how to start practicing as a consultant, this is a step-by-step guide to seeing if you have what it takes to get started as a consultant.

Some Useful Web Sites

ConsultingCafe.com. A hub of the consulting community, this site offers a wide variety of articles, forums, and other resources to help you succeed in your consultancy career, whatever your industry of expertise.

Guru.com. This site acts as a clearinghouse for consultants and employers. Projects are posted ranging from Web site design and legal work to writing and graphic design.

Institute of Management Consultants USA: www.imcusa.org. This is the site for the preeminent professional association for management and business consultants.

Books on Buying a Franchise

Franchise Bible: How to Buy a Franchise or Franchise Your Own Business by Erwin J. Keup and Peter Keup. Entrepreneur Press, 2012, seventh edition. This popular and proven reference guide has been updated thoroughly and includes a wide array of real-life examples of franchise ownership, as well as checklists to help prevent you from wasting valuable time and money.

The Franchise MBA: Mastering the Four Essential Steps to Owning a Franchise by Nick Neonakis, with Sagar Rambhia and Aditya Rengaswamy. CreateSpace Independent Publishing, 2013. This book brings together all the disparate pieces of information you'll need to know to make franchise ownership work. With insights from respected franchise owners, this book includes tips on finding the right franchise, management, in addition to legal and financial pointers.

Some Useful Web Sites

Franchise.com. This site provides information on buying domestic and international franchises, finding real estate, and financing your franchise.

FranChoice.com. A free service for entrepreneurs, FranChoice offers information and expert advice on buying a franchise. They will guide you through the franchise consultation process, choosing a franchise that best suits you, and will get you started on the research needed to begin ownership of your own franchise.

FranNet.com. A complimentary service that will connect you with local franchise coaches who will help you find the best franchise opportunity in your location of choice. With access to locally based expertise, they can help ensure your likelihood of success in franchise entrepreneurship.

Books on Buying a Business

Buying a Business That Makes You Rich by John Martinka. Book Publishers Network, 2013. A great primer to buying your own business and "escaping the corporate rat race." Inside, you will find different proven formulas and strategies to choose the right business, avoid overpaying, and how to turn your business into a stable and lucrative source of income.

How to Buy and/or Sell a Small Business for Maximum Profit: A Step-by-Step Guide, by Rene V. Richards, updated by Constance H. Marse. Atlantic Publishing, 2013, second edition. This book is geared toward the novice entrepreneur who wants to buy or sell a small business. Topics are comprehensive and include raising capital, using discounted cash flow, and understanding buyouts, letters of intent, legal and tax concerns, and contracts.

The Website Investor: The Guide to Buying an Online Website Business for Passive Income by Jeff Hunt. Morgan James Publishing, 2015. Based on the premise that savvy businesspeople know to never start from scratch, this book tells you how you can purchase a Web site that is already making money and use it to become a passive supplemental income or your primary source of income.

A Useful Web Site

BizBuySell.com. This site lists thousands of established businesses for sale, forms, checklists, and interactive worksheets, plus recommendations of articles, books, and Web sites to help you buy a business.

Books on Freelancing

The Freelancer's Bible: Everything You Need to Know to Have the Career of Your Dreams—On Your Terms by Sara Horowitz. Workman Publishing, 2012. Written by the authority on freelancing, MacArthur "Genius" Fellow, and founder of both the national Freelancers Union and the Freelancers Insurance Company, this book will help you either learn what freelancing is all about, or how to grow and expand. There's a thorough guide to every practical detail and challenge of being a successful freelancer.

My So-Called Freelance Life: How to Survive and Thrive as a Creative Professional for Hire by Michelle Goodman. Seal Press, 2008. A classic that will always be worth the read, this book provides a candid look into the freelancing world that everyone who is thinking about doing it for themselves should be aware of. Though geared toward women, it's an invaluable resource for all.

Some Useful Web Sites

Elance.com. You can create a profile for free and start looking for offers right away, or you can have their system start doing it for you. An added bonus is that they will take care of all the things that take away from your productivity, like paperwork, invoicing, and payment.

Freelancer.com. One of the best and biggest sites around, Freelancer .com has jobs available for a huge variety of categories. Getting a job on Freelancer.com is based on a bidding system. Once the offer is published, you bid for work, set a price, present your skills, and promote your services. So, it's all up to you.

Freelancer's Union: www.freelancersunion.org. Freelancing has become so popular, there's even a freelancers' union. Membership enables freelancers to receive information about money, taxes, marketing, and time management as well as receive discounts on health insurance, disability benefits, and a range of products and services.

Upwork.com. With more than one hundred thousand freelance opportunities posted monthly, there is always an abundance of long- or short-term projects to get involved with, covering a wide array of skill levels. Choose how you get paid, get rated for good work, and keep a steady stream of freelance work coming to you.

Books on Marketing and Selling How-tos

Guerrilla Marketing in 30 Days by Jay Conrad Levinson and Al Lautenslager. Entrepreneur Press, 2014. This book shows marketers how to focus on their marketing goals to maximize profits. Learn from real-life examples, success stories, and proven core concepts, along with daily exercises to increase profits, cut costs, and gain new clients.

The New Rules of Marketing & PR: How to Use Social Media, Online Video, Mobile Applications, Blogs, News Releases & Viral Marketing to Reach Buyers Directly by David Meerman Scott. John Wiley & Sons, 2013. A great guide for the technical novice on the basics of digital marketing and ways to harness the Internet to lead customers into the buying process.

Books on Starting Your Own Business

Entrepreneurial StrengthsFinder by Jim Clifton and Sangeeta Bharadwaj Badal. Gallup Press, 2014. Gallup's CEO, Clifton, and Badal, the primary researcher for Gallup's Entrepreneurship and Job

Creation initiative, build on Gallup's incredibly successful Strengths-Finder 2.0 in this book. They explain the ten talents that successful entrepreneurs possess, in a language that helps people understand which areas they are talented in and the ones they are not drawn to.

The Small Business Bible: Everything You Need to Know to Succeed in Your Small Business by Steven D. Strauss. John Wiley & Sons, 2012, third edition. A popular guide on building a successful small business whether you're a budding entrepreneur or seasoned businessperson. Filled with tips, insider information, stories, and proven secrets of success, this book is vital to small-business owners everywhere.

Small Time Operator: How to Start Your Own Business, Keep Your Books, Pay Your Taxes, and Stay Out of Trouble by Bernard B. Kamoroff. Taylor Trade Publishing, 2013, thirteenth edition. Perfect for the small-business owner, freelancer, and independent contractor, this is one of the most popular start-up guides available. It takes you through the entire process of starting and establishing a business, financing, hiring, bookkeeping, taxes, and more.

The Startup Owner's Manual: The Step-by-Step Guide for Building a Great Company by Steve Blank and Bob Dorf. K&S Ranch, 2012. Offers detailed, step-by-step instructions on building successful, scalable, and profitable businesses. Used by the National Science Foundation, Stanford, Berkeley, Columbia, and more than one hundred other leading universities, you'll find valuable charts, diagrams, graphs, and checklists to help you build a powerful and successful business.

Zero to One: Notes on Startups, or How to Build the Future by Peter Thiel, with Blake Masters. Crown Business, 2014. This bestselling book puts forward the idea that innovation and progress can be made in any industry or area of business by simply learning to think for one's self. An optimistic view of the future of progress, success in the future is all about finding value in unexpected places.

Books on Writing a Business Plan

Business Plan Writing Guide: How to Write a Successful & Sustainable Business Plan in Under 3 Hours by ClydeBank Media. ClydeBank Media, 2014. In just fifty-six pages ClydeBank Media lays out the steps to writing a business plan in a straightforward and clear style.

Writing a Convincing Business Plan by Arthur R. DeThomas, Stephanie Derammelaere, and Steven Fox. Barron's Educational Series, 2015, fourth edition. This book shows how to organize and write a logical, business-savvy, and professional business plan that can be presented to banks and potential investors.

Some Useful Web Sites

Bplans.com. In addition to advice on topics ranging from starting a business to helpful business software to reading lists for effective start-ups, this site includes a variety of sample business plans you can search that match your business.

Entrepreneur magazine: www.entrepreneur.com. This site is rich with resources for new business ideas, writing a marketing plan, raising financing, and growing your business.

Inc. magazine: *www.Inc.com*. This site contains information about how to plan and start a small business and advice for small-business owners about such topics as technology, hiring and motivating employees, marketing, and customer service.

LegalZoom.com. A site that offers low-cost legal document services for incorporations, LLCs, trademarks, patents, and copyrights.

MyLLCAgreement.com. A site that offers free to low-cost LLC agreements along with phone or online support for any entrepreneur or business owner.

Success magazine: *www.Success.com*. This site contains trends, tips, and ideas for entrepreneurs as well as profiles of successful entrepreneurs.

US Small Business Administration: www.sba.gov. A vast site with information on starting a business, financing, business opportunities, disaster assistance, local offices, SCORE resources in your area, and more.

Chapter 10: One Toe in the Retirement Pool

Books

The 5 Years Before You Retire: Retirement Planning When You Need It the Most by Emily Guy Birken. Adams Media, 2014. Most Americans don't realize until they're in their sixties that they haven't put away enough money to retire comfortably. This helpful guide will take you through all the major financial, medical, and familial decisions you'll need to make to help you reach your retirement goals.

Get What's Yours: The Secrets to Maxing Out Your Social Security by Laurence J. Kotlikoff, Philip Moeller, and Paul Solman. Simon & Schuster, 2015. Social Security is important to everyone entering retirement, and this book will show you how to maximize your benefits to the fullest potential, and also how to avoid several costly mistakes that not many know about.

How to Retire Happy: The 12 Most Important Decisions You Must Make Before You Retire by Stan Hinden. McGraw-Hill, 2013, fourth edition. This book helps you make all the right decisions you need to ensure a happy retirement. Organized in an easy to digest step-by-step fashion, everyone nearing retirement is sure to get some useful information from this very popular and recommended book.

Life Reimagined: Discovering Your New Life Possibilities by Richard J. Leider and Alan M. Webber. Berrett-Koehler Publishers, 2013. Leider and Webber explain how the old model of retirement is dead and useless in a world where we are living longer and demanding more of ourselves no matter our age. They then focus on possibilities in life and how to approach transitions.

Revolutionary Retirement: What's Next for YOU? by Catherine Allen, Nancy Bearg, Rita Foley, and Jaye Smith. Reboot Partners LLC, 2014. Information-packed and filled with stories, this is a comforting guide written for baby boomers eyeing the next phase of reinvention.

What's Next? Finding Your Passion and Your Dream Job in Your Forties, Fifties, and Beyond by Kerry Hannon. Berkley, 2014, revised and updated edition. Filled with advice, resources, and stories about real people who have chosen to change their careers at a later age. Hannon is a journalist who has written about "second acts for years."

Some Useful Web Sites

AARP.org. From America's leading organization for people age fifty and older, this site provides information and education about health and wellness, leisure and fun, legislative issues, life transitions, money, work, volunteering, and computers and technology.

Encore.org. This organization seeks to utilize the talents, skills, and expertise of those in midlife and beyond with the goal of helping to improve communities and the world through the creation of programs and resources that directly benefit society.

FeistySideOfFifty.com. A fun Web site that celebrates the remarkable generation of baby-boomer women. Filled with inspiring stories and links to engaging media, this site is definitely worth a visit.

Money.com. In addition to covering many retirement topics such as choosing appropriate investment vehicles, setting up family trusts, and understanding the roles of pensions, 401(k)s, and IRAs, this site offers retirement savings and cost-of-living calculators, and a tool for finding the best place to retire.

Quicken.com. This site contains general financial information and a good selection of pages on retirement basics such as 401(k)s, pension plans, IRAs, Social Security, and a retirement planner as well as the special topics of taking care of aging parents and planning for inflation. It also offers software for retirement planning.

Social Security Retirement Planner: www.ssa.gov. This government site provides information on eligibility factors affecting retirement benefits, options available as you near retirement, and several benefit calculators using different retirement scenarios.

Chapter 11: The Eleven Keys to Success

Books

Decisive: How to Make Better Choices in Life and Work by Chip Heath and Dan Heath. Crown Business, 2013. The Heath brothers address a fact that many of us already know: that when it comes to decision making, our brains can be rather flawed. Acknowledging this, this book aims at helping us to stop agonizing over decisions, how to make group decisions while avoiding politics, and how to never miss opportunities by floundering.

Flourish: A Visionary New Understanding of Happiness and Well-being by Martin E. P. Seligman. Atria Books, 2012, reprint. Psychologist Martin Seligman, the author of the classic book *Learned Optimism: How to Change Your Mind and Your Life* puts forth a powerful idea of what well-being actually is. This book is all about creating the permanent building blocks for a life of profound fulfillment.

Following Through: A Revolutionary New Model for Finishing Whatever You Start by Steve Levinson and Pete Greider. CreateSpace Independent Publishing, 2015, third edition. This book teaches different ways to understand and handle your good intentions as well as make things happen.

The Gifts of Imperfection: Let Go of Who You Think You're Supposed to Be and Embrace Who You Are by Brené Brown. Hazelden, 2010. In this book, Brown shares ten guideposts on the power of Wholehearted living; a way of engaging with the world from a place of worthiness. Perfect for building the confidence you need to get out into the world and tackle any challenges that you may face.

How We Decide by Jonah Lehrer. Houghton Mifflin Harcourt, 2009. This book is an insightful read about the science of decision making.

The Power of Habit: Why We Do What We Do in Life and Business by Charles Duhigg. Random House, 2014. The exciting argument of this book is that the key to losing weight, exercising, being more productive, finding success at work, engaging socially, and many other things, is understanding how habits work. A fantastic resource for developing the perseverance needed for success and fulfillment.

Some Useful Web Sites and Blogs

Addicted2Success.com. This site is dedicated to achieving success in all areas of business. It features articles on entrepreneurship, motivation, start-ups, and life in general; also includes links to several podcasts.

TheChangeBlog.com. A community of more than fifty thousand people who come together to share their stories and experiences of creating positive change in their lives. Full of inspiration and practical advice on how to make the changes you seek in your own life.

HelpGuide.org. This comprehensive nonprofit Web site with the tagline "Understand, Prevent & Resolve Life's Challenges" has hundreds of articles on topics such as humor, creativity, communication, and many of the other Eleven Keys to Success.

PickTheBrain.com. Popular blog on personal development and growth, with a focus on motivation, productivity, and confidence.

Psychtests Test Yourself: http://testyourself.psychtests.com. This Web site has a multitude of tests, including a thirty-five-minute test to assess your emotional intelligence.

StevenAitchison.co.uk/blog. A popular blog dedicated to the notion that changing your thoughts can change your life. Focuses on psychology, personal development, lifestyle, relationships, health, spirituality, and business.

Chapter 12: Job Search—the Nuts and Bolts

Books on Job Search How-tos

How to Get a Job in 30 Days or Less: Discover Hiring Secrets and Job Getting Tips & Strategies to Find the Job You Desire by George Egbuonu. Helping Feet, 2013. Tips for landing a job by giving the reader hiring secrets on applying and interviewing for any job, regardless of qualifications, education, or experience.

The Job Search Solution: The Ultimate System for Finding a Great Job Now! by Tony Beshara. AMACOM, 2012, second edition. Addresses the major concerns of people searching for a job in today's difficult job market, including advice for those who have gaps in employment, were fired from their last job, or are looking for a career change. Features interactive exercises, real-life examples, and practical do's and don'ts.

Job Searching with Social Media for Dummies by Joshua Waldman. John Wiley & Sons, 2013. Take full advantage of the proven power of social networks to leverage your contacts into job leads. Learn how to build and maintain your online presence and how to use the power of personal branding.

Knock 'em Dead 2015: The Ultimate Job Search Guide 2015 by Martin Yate. Adams Media, 2014. This book has been praised as one of the most comprehensive career books on the market. It is filled with interviewing strategies, Internet resources, and tools for helping job applicants stand out.

The 2-Hour Job Search: Using Technology to Get the Right Job Faster by Steve Dalton. Ten Speed Press, 2012. This book teaches its readers how to leverage the power of technology to get an interview and find a job smarter and faster. Tips on how to use the power of Google, LinkedIn, alumni databases, and more to secure an interview with only two hours of effort.

Team Up! Find a Better Job Faster with a Job Search Work Team by Orville Pierson. Highly Effective Job Search, 2014, fifth edition. This is a guide for forming and running a job search group, often a proven formula for job seekers who support each other with their job search challenges.

What Color Is Your Parachute? 2015: A Practical Manual for Job-Hunters and Career-Changers by Richard N. Bolles. Ten Speed Press, 2014. First published in 1970 and updated annually, this book remains a classic in the field.

A Useful Web Site

The Five O'Clock Club: www.fiveoclockclub.com. The Five O'Clock
Club is a national outplacement and career-counseling network
with certified career counselors across the United States.

Books on Branding

BrandingPays: The Five-Step System to Reinvent Your Personal Brand
by Karen Kang. BrandingPays Media, 2013. The only way to
stand out from the crowd in today's connected and competitive
world is to focus on your personal brand. This is a practical
guide to strategic personal branding that will help you refocus
your skills and experience so that you are the best candidate for
the job.

Personal Branding for Dummies by Susan Chritton. John Wiley &
Sons, 2014, second edition. Find a competitive edge by marketing your skills and personality. This is a clear-cut guide to help
yourself stand out from the competition by establishing a clear
and concise image, reputation, and status in the digital world.

Promote Yourself: The New Rules for Career Success by Dan Schawbel.
St. Martin's Press, 2013. A research-driven approach to building
a personal brand, this book offers not only ways to build an
online presence but also how to build your personal communication and networking skills, with advice on how to do so from an
insider's perspective.

Reinventing You: Define Your Brand, Imagine Your Future by Dorie
Clark. Harvard Business School Publishing, 2013. A step-by-step
guide to help you identify your unique strengths and build a
personal brand that communicates your expertise and what it is
that you are able to contribute.

Some Useful Web Sites

About.me. A sleek and minimal site that acts as a digital business
card with the added benefit of being interactive. With easy-to-use
design tools, you can set your page exactly how you want it to

look, setting the tone for your branding message. You can include a photo of yourself, some personal info, a short summary of who you are, and links to all of the social media sites on which you have a presence.

BrandYourself.com. A Web service for individuals or for businesses that helps control what people see when they search for you on the Internet. Helps clean up search results to make sure people see what you want them to see, offering both free and paid services.

Mention: https://en.mention.com. Allows you to set up a list of keywords and topics that you would like to constantly be listening for on the Web. When something relevant to your personal branding strategy is mentioned, you receive an alert and are able to quickly react or respond, ensuring you have your finger on the pulse of your industry and that your voice is heard with as much reach as possible.

Books on Interviewing

15 Minutes to a Better Interview: What I Wish Every Job Candidate Knew by Russell Tuckerton. CreateSpace Independent Publishing, 2013. Learn from the author's twenty years of experience conducting interviews and find out what mistakes you may be making that are costing you the job you want.

Knock 'em Dead Job Interview: How to Turn Job Interviews into Job Offers by Martin Yate. Adams Media, 2013. Using his twenty-five years of experience, Yate tells you proven ways to get noticed in an interview. Rather than memorizing answers to interview questions, you should understand the thoughts behind the questions. By learning what the interviewer is really trying to find out about you, you're sure to give the answers that others will miss.

How to Win Friends and Influence People by Dale Carnegie. CreateSpace Independent Publishing, 2015. This time-honored classic—first published in 1936—is a must-read for anyone stepping into an interview. Being prepared to answer all the questions and being able to talk at length about your qualifications and experience are important, but it's the spaces in between these moments that may make all the difference. Show up with an electrifying personality that the whole office will remember and talk about afterward, and you'll be sure to stand out from everyone else.

101 Great Answers to the Toughest Interview Questions by Ron Fry. Cengage Learning PTR, 2009, sixth edition. A popular bestseller, this is a great read for those looking for some direct answers on how to navigate your way through some of the most infamous interview questions, such as the always popular "What's your greatest weakness?"

60 Seconds & You're Hired! by Robin Ryan. Penguin Books, 2016, updated edition. In this bestselling guide, Ryan provides concise advice and easy techniques for mastering an interview.

Some Useful Web Sites

CareerBuilder.com. One of the largest and most popular job search sites, you're sure to find some leads in no time. You can upload a résumé that can be searched by companies, so if you're a fit for a job, they'll contact you. Be sure to check out the resources page, where you can find a wealth of useful information about almost anything career-related, sortable by industry and job phase.

Craigslist.org. This Web site is a centralized network of online communities featuring free online classified ads with sections devoted to jobs, résumés, housing, and for-sale services.

Glassdoor.com. A Web site where employees and former employees anonymously review companies and their management on corporate culture, compensation, and other insights.

Indeed.com. This site aggregates job postings from job sites, newspapers, associations, and company career pages. Indeed.com also releases industry trends to help job seekers and employers navigate the job market.

JibberJobber.com. An online tool that enables you to track jobs, network contacts, monitor the strength of your relationships, keep tabs on specific companies you want to work for, and view a multitude of videos on relevant topics.

JobDig.com. This employment media company publishes local editions in more than fourteen states in print and on the Web.

TheLadders.com. This job site allows job seekers, for a monthly subscription fee, to search for jobs that pay $100,000 or more in sales, marketing, finance, human resources, law, technology, and operations.

LinkUp.com. This job search engine only indexes jobs from over twenty thousand company Web sites, giving job seekers access to the purest jobs on the Web—direct from the source.

Monster.com. This is a "monster" site with more than three thousand pages of career advice, résumés, and salary information, as well as a vast job-posting database. Additional features include opportunities for senior executives, advice on relocating, and a database for contractors.

Books on Résumé Writing

How to Write a Resume (Interview Tips and Job Interview Questions): Learn How to Craft a Professional Resume to Find Your Dream Job Easily by Richard Forbes. CreateSpace Independent Publishing, 2015, third edition. This book covers every element of creating an effective résumé as well as offering résumé and cover letter templates and sample résumés.

Knock 'em Dead Resumes: A Killer Resume Gets More Interviews! by Martin Yate. Adams Media, 2014, eleventh edition. This book has been a bestseller for more than a decade, and this updated version includes new examples of résumés and a new "before" and "after" section. It features the latest information on online postings, e-mail techniques, and follow-up strategies.

The Resume Writing Handbook: The Essential Guide to Writing Resumes by Jason Wright. Howlin Publishing, 2015. Kindle version. Wright likens an effective résumé to an art masterpiece. It requires a lot of work to create and to make you stand out so you get interviews.

Some Useful Web Sites

TheMuse.com. Designed for younger adults and college students who are in need of career help, The Muse offers free advice on résumé and cover letter writing, general career advice, job skills, and actually finding a job that is right for you.

Talentral.com. Allows members to maximize their efforts in starting a career by combining career management, personal branding, media presentations, and résumé information in one central place that can be searched by potential employers, letting the job come looking for you.

VisualCV.com. This site lets you easily create multiple résumés with professional and modern design options, and track e-mail opens, résumé views, and downloads, providing insights into your résumé performance.

Workfolio.com. Takes your résumé well beyond the traditional format and updates it into a fully digital experience, turning your résumé, CV, and experience into a personal Web site. Allows your résumé to come up in Web searches and gives potential employers access to blogs, articles, and any other social presence you have designed to build your personal brand.

Books on Networking

How to Be a Power Connector: The 5+50+100 Rule for Turning Your Business Network into Profits by Judy Robinett. McGraw-Hill, 2014. Helps you create a "power grid" of connections that will greatly accelerate your personal and professional achievement. By practicing strategic relationship planning, you can easily get the most value from any of your networks.

How to Write a KILLER LinkedIn Profile . . . And 18 Mistakes to Avoid: Updated for 2015 by Brenda Bernstein. Wise Media Group, 2014, eleventh edition. Great advice for those who are new to LinkedIn, or for those who have been there since the beginning. Features eighteen of the most common mistakes people make on their profile, and how to fix them.

Networking for People Who Hate Networking: A Field Guide for Introverts, the Overwhelmed, and the Underconnected by Devora Zack. Berrett-Koehler, 2010. Many people shudder at the thought of networking, for a number of reasons. This book helps you harness what are usually considered networking weaknesses, and turn them into strengths. Great for those you are truly introverts, or those who want to try a new networking strategy.

Networking Is Not Working: Stop Collecting Business Cards and Start Making Meaningful Connections by Derek Coburn. IdeaPress, 2014. Born from the author's frustration with attending countless networking events with little to no real results, this book offers fresh and unconventional strategies for growing and nurturing a powerful network.

Never Eat Alone: And Other Secrets to Success, One Relationship at a Time by Keith Ferrazzi. Crown Business, 2014, expanded and updated. Ferrazzi distinguishes his unique and counterintuitive perspective on networking from the usual concept of networking involving generic handshakes and handing out business cards.

Some Useful Web Sites

LinkedIn.com. The preeminent professional social networking platform, LinkedIn has become an essential part of how people network in nearly every profession and industry. Members can search for jobs, join industry- and function-related groups, and submit job applications, as well as endorse skills and write recommendations for those people they are connected to on the site.

Meetup.com. This site allows users to create their own professional networks, or join existing ones. The major benefit of Meetup is that it encourages in-person meetings, while still allowing for online connections. An incredible opportunity to rapidly expand

your networking, Meetup is an easy-to-use option for professionals in every industry.

Quora.com. A question-and-answer site, Quora allows its users to
create, edit, answer, and organize a variety of questions from its
community of users. Well-received answers can be a great way
to build your personal brand online, and also to discover industry leaders and professional peers with whom to connect.

Xing.com. A platform for business networking, Xing offers profiles,
forums, groups, and more. Used by people in more than two
hundred countries, it stands apart from other social networks
in that it offers an ambassador program for each city or region
with enough members in which the ambassador will hold a local
event where people can meet in person to discuss business opportunities.

A Book on Search Firms

Everything You Wish to Ask a Headhunter by Steven Pang and Adrian
Tan. Candid Creation Publishing, 2013. With in-depth global
experience in executive search, recruiting, and staffing, Pang and
Tan share answers to questions such as "How do I get on a headhunter's radar?" "Why do I need an elevator pitch?" and "How
should I handle typical interview questions?"

A Useful Blog

Ask the Headhunter: http://corcodilos.com/blog. Popular longtime
blogger Nick Corcodilos has many years of experience in helping
people break into the careers that they want by offering insider
information that isn't told to you by others. Headhunters know
how to bring companies the people they're looking for, and Nick
can tell you how to be one of those people.

An Interesting Survey

JobVite Social Recruiting Survey. http://www.jobvite.com/wpcon
tent/uploads/2014/10/Jobvite_SocialRecruiting_Survey2014.pdf.
This survey, completed by nearly 1,900 recruiting and human

resources professionals spanning across industries, reveals hiring trends in the areas of social recruiting, sourcing, and talent acquisition.

A Useful Web Site
Career Thought Leaders: www.careerthoughtleaders.com/white paper/. This is a comprehensive report of career trends culled from a Global Brainstorming Day in 2015.

Index

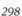